CHANGING ART
CHANGING MAN
CHANGING ART
CHANGING MAN
CHANGING ART
CHANGING MAN

CHANGING ART

CHANGING MAN

BY

DAVID MANDEL

HORIZON PRESS   NEW YORK

For Eda Lou Walton and Marianna Byram, gallant wives.

Gift500/5/17/71

CONTENTS

ACKNOWLEDGMENTS

This book represents an effort begun long ago as an undergraduate at college to make for art in the future a place at the center of man's consciousness, the intrusive constant factor in a growing and finer biological response to the world. Any center of value and purpose is to be preferred to none, but art in its evolutionary aspect is one possibility surely.

My thanks are due primarily to N. Walter Haring, my classmate at Princeton, 1919, and onetime head of the Barnard College Fine Arts Department, who was of a remarkable and trustworthy sensitivity to the old and the new, and a superb questioner; to Gerta Prosser for help with the text; to Thomas C. Cochran of the University of Pennsylvania History Department for many fruitful quarrels; to Kenneth Burke, old friend, fine mind and generous opponent.   — D.M.

I

ART
AND THE
EVOLUTIONARY
ADVANCE

C H A P T E R O N E

"The appreciation of beauty of form and colour, as well as of sound and rhythm was acquired as the result of the cultivation of these powers of discrimination, the evolution of which I have been trying to interpret as the outcome of the development of the abilities conferred by stereoscopic vision. The further investigation of these evolutionary processes will, I believe, afford the interpretation of the biological meaning of aesthetics."

G. Elliot Smith
The Evolution of Man

We begin with the dance of the electron and end with the dance of the imagination. We begin with "inert" matter, to which we are related, and end with creative powers of specially endowed human beings, the artists. Evolution, the miracle of growing sensitivity and increasing consciousness, has led us so inevitably to art that in a certain view it may finally be through aesthetics that we interpret the meaning of biology.

Man displays his creative powers through art. Nature displays hers through evolution. The two are intertwined and reciprocal. For art changes man and man changes art.

The evolutionary span, from the area of least to highest awareness, divides into three major sectors with two enormous gaps in between. The earliest, inanimate period of the earth is now believed to have started some five billion years ago. Then about seven hundred million years ago, there was a leap into the animate. Scientists are still seeking to discover just how this leap was made. The exploration of large molecules and viruses will no doubt some day yield up the secret of this mutation. One remembers a great biologist, Edwin Grant Conklin, telling his class at Princeton some fifty years ago that forty years before that he had made a bet that life would by then be created in the laboratory. The gap has not been easy to bridge.

Once life began, it proliferated into myriads of creatures, some of whose evolutionary histories have been well charted. First came plants, with the ability to reproduce and with a life cycle, but with no central nervous system. Then animals appeared, and this is the period when sensuosity and feeling began, and the first central nervous system.

Then there was another gap, and this too science is still trying to bridge. The leap from animals to men is still mysterious, though part of the progression is known. It has been established that roughly 100,000 years ago animals reached a higher threshold of sensitivity with the emergence of a creature possessing a degree of consciousness that opened out to him a new world of meanings and values. Man is the first symbol-using and artifact-making animal. Words made communication possible on a level far beyond that of his predecessors. In him first appeared "the power of the mind over the possibilities of things," Wallace Stevens' phrase for the imagination.[1] Teilhard de Chardin, referring to this transformation, chooses *reflection* as the central phenomenon, calling it "the power acquired by a consciousness to turn in upon itself, to take possession of itself *as an object* endowed with its own particular conscience and value: no longer merely to know, but to know oneself . . . to know that one knows."[2]

Research into brain functions and in genetics promises to explain this enormous leap into self-consciousness, as well as the hereditary mechanism that has maintained it. Indeed, it has been said that the next century will see discoveries in biology comparable to those made in physics during the last hundred years.

Matter has evolved toward sensitivity, then, through three levels: inanimate, living, self-conscious. Or, if you will, imagine first a world of purely formal mathematical relationships. From these somehow came movement, feeling, sensuosity. Then last, in a comparatively recent progression, a third manifestation grew out of the formal and the sensuous: a mind capable of self-consciousness, reflection, evaluation, symbol-making. Through these

[1] Wallace Stevens, *The Necessary Angel* (Vintage Book, 1967), p. 136.
[2] Teilhard de Chardin, *The Phenomenon of Man* (Harper & Row, 1959), p. 165.

plateaus we have come to man, the animal with imagination. Is the miraculous pageant finished at this point? Or is there justification for faith that man's consciousness is still growing, and that there are further levels to reach from this platform?

It seems entirely possible that human beings can now consciously foster and hasten the process that has been developing unconsciously over millions of years. Blindly the forces of nature have reached steadily upward along the ladder of awareness. Not just the fittest have survived: the most sensitive have shown a surprising ability to endure. Not only the brute rock, the giant redwood, the elephant — but frail flower, delicate mammal, and vulnerable man, these too have come through.

From what we know of the past, which is now considerable, there is no sure evidence that the process has ended with the appearance of man. There is indeed one bit of evidence that evolution continues, namely, man's creative imagination. Here is a tool that may take man to still higher levels. And by this we do not mean merely the aid that the imagination gives science, but also its function in art, where it is able to seize all the elements that have comprised our sensuous and conceptual evolution, and embody them in concrete artifacts. These in turn provide experiences that extend our awareness of ourselves and our destiny.

All art without exception has a base of formal relationships such as those that run through the whole of nature. These refer back to our origins in inanimate matter, and we respond to them from deep and even dormant layers of our sensibility. Art's second element, sensuosity —

14

living rhythm, texture, color — quickens our own sensuous responses as we receive it through eyes and ears. Lastly it has something to convey to our minds — concepts, ideas, evaluation, associations — something recent in biological history and peculiar to man alone. This last element, which is present in all great art, draws on our newest human faculties and is what makes art a tool not just for our pleasure but for our further advance as well. It might be called the seed that keeps our "humanness" growing.

Like the embryo in its mother, the man-made artifact shows to some extent signs from each level of our evolutionary past: the inanimate, animate and meaningful. Here perhaps the veneration of the artist will eventually find a scientific basis. His power to unite in one small object the three levels of nature that mark the ascent of man puts the artist at the peak of the pyramid of awareness. His imagination is life's topmost performance and his artifacts may prove to be a portent of a development yet to come. We are still somewhat in the dark as to the causes of mutations, as life interacts with nature. What happens when man interacts with a work of art is also a mystery. Giving it a biological meaning may involve imprecision as long as mystery remains, yet it may shed some light on the nature of man and art, and the significance of the aesthetic experience.

Since art reflects not only man's primitive origins but also his mind, it is not too fantastic to see in great works adumbrations of our biological future or, to put it in another way, a spiritual quality in the making. Great works of art, organized by superior organisms, show us a way of seeing or hearing that we could not otherwise achieve. One might call an art museum or concert hall a spiritual gymnasium where we stretch our consciousness on constructions made by the artist. We begin to use deeper, unfamiliar layers of reception that lie buried under the normal functions of the life of our day. Each of these constructions, or aesthetic instruments, is composed of the three elements we have seen to be involved in our ascent from inanimate matter: formal patterns; animal sensuosity; and finally, abstract concepts, association, evaluation. These elements are named in art: *form, feeling* and *meaning.*

The form, or basic element of a painting, is often described as the relationship between the parts or the arrangement of masses. Such relationships are found as patterns throughout nature. Even inanimate matter evidences rhythm on a general mathematical scheme of repetition and juxtaposition. This may come from some primal dynamic pulse involved in the origins of our world. These very ancient geometric elements in nature can be analyzed, and it is here that scientific logic yields its richest results. Rules have been discovered and universal modes and motifs recognized.

But attempts by scientists, notably psychologists, to invade and analyze the three-tiered work of art, the wholly new thing, have been notably unsuccessful. Though the tools of science can measure eye and ear reactions and electrical waves in the brain, they are still too blunt to chart the limitless complexities of the individual imagination.

Art's second level, the area of the living and the

16

sensuous, is composed of energy, movement, color, texture, warmth — all qualities associated with the pulse and breath of animal life that make us *feel* the work of art and respond to it pleasurably. On this level the artist takes the ancient geometric forms and gives them his own dynamic rhythm and equilibrium. Many works stop at this level and yet find their place in museums. A simple undecorated vase may not arouse our deepest emotions but it can be enjoyed in terms of its rhythm, texture, composition, vitality. By the same token a painting existing only on the first two aesthetic levels — that is, without recognizable meaning — can give some pleasure, as long as the dynamic energy of the artist has been sufficient to move our senses to a response.

Pleasures of the senses are common, but when do we call a pleasure aesthetic? Both formal and sensuous elements are necessary if the painting, sculpture, music, or literary work is to provide an aesthetic experience. A square has form but lacks sensuosity. A splash of color has sensuosity but lacks form. To a few — the mathematicians — purely formal arrangements have a semblance of aesthetic appeal, and to many a color alone will give pleasure. But when the quality of sensuousness is provided entirely by the observer, as in the case of the mathematician, we would hesitate to call the exchange between object and audience aesthetic. No mathematical formula awaits us in the museum and no simple daub of color. The two must be combined. Complexity is a necessity in art as well as life. Our biological equipment, our sensory receptors that have been developing since evolution began, demand it.

17

So many efforts at definitions have failed that there is a strong reaction against setting any limit to what shall be called art. Our analogy from biology does give us limits, but in no way precludes experimentation. To ask that at least two elements out of three shall be required before we consider an object to have aesthetic use is not too confining. Between the mathematical formula and the inchoate heap of matter or the color splash there is ample ground for the artist.

The third element in a work of art is the human one. The greatest art contains meaning and human significance, given concretion in the two biologically older elements of form and sensuosity. As we have said, man's consciousness of his world and of his own existence and death added a new dimension to the animal. One way that art conveys meaning is through imitation of the tangible objective reality we inhabit. Emotional reality provides meaning too — sadness, fear, pain or joy in a face or gesture, the nostalgia in a landscape, the exaltation in a musical passage, the despair in a lyric verse, the tentative gentleness in the drawing of a rabbit. Meaning, associations, concepts relate the work of art to humanity and give it the final complexity that fulfills our needs. A vase, no matter how appealing to the senses, can never have the power of a Rembrandt. When, as in abstract expressionism for instance, the human emotion or idea is largely omitted, then the deposit of meaning needed to complete the two elements, form and feeling, is very thin, and the work suffers some dimunition.

Indeed, one might go further and say that content, or meaning, is itself another kind of form. We can, for

18

example, imagine a painting in which a gesture by a human being outweighs by virtue of its significance heavier counterposed objects. This actually occurs in the Giottos of the Arena Chapel. A pair of eyes filled with anguish can outbalance a larger area of color. And when one speaks of occult balance in Goya's picture of the bull set against a wide section of space, what is this but meaning counterweighing formal elements of greater size. This specific gravity factor of meaning can play an important part, though it is unfashionable today, and artists, fortified by critics and for a number of reasons to be discussed later, have downgraded its function and value. This is of course not to say that we have not had some very skillful and stimulating abstract art.

It is true that it makes the artist's job more difficult and demands more capacity to unite the three elements instead of the two. But the rejection or submergence of the human ideational and emotional element makes for a blandness or a perverse obscurity that reduces the intellectual as well as the emotional experience of the beholder. To best call up and exercise the buried powers of reception and feeling that each of us carries in us from our past, the artist needs to attack on all three levels. A complex, many-faceted consciousness is the inheritance of the human race. As Teilhard de Chardin writes: "In its own way, matter has obeyed from the beginning that great law of biology to which we shall have to recur time and time again, the law of 'complexification.' "[1] Great art follows the same law.

[1] *Ibid.*, p. 48.

The professor of art history, who is not dealing with present trends as much as with the past, plays perhaps a more important role than the critic; his interpretations are likely to influence thousands of young minds toward new and fresh perception. He is apt to mingle rather than make clear distinctions between the separate values of the three elements — form, sensuousness and meaning. It is possible that by separating and identifying them more clearly he could give the student a deeper comprehension of the link between art and our biological selves. The emphasis on form, as the oldest aesthetic element and essential to all creation, would then take on its proper significance. The sensuous ingredient, also essential, could also be more clearly understood. Poussin, for example, magnificent for his rhythmic form had a weak color sense and though he was a great painter he was diminished by that lack. In the same way, the lack of the third element, human meaning, as we observe it in recent abstract painting and sculpture, will quite probably in the long view diminish the art of this century. Complete elimination of any one of the three elements is bound to lower the rank of the work eventually. For this we have only to look at the weaker works of Monet and the deficiency of form so obvious in his late haystacks and sun-drenched cathedrals. The artist needs to operate on all three levels. That is what makes for a good gestalt — a form-pervaded image that impresses itself readily and deeply on our total receptor system and effects a reorganization there.

What do we know biologically about these receptors, these areas of the brain so often dormant and so essential to the aesthetic experience? Obviously they exist, but are called upon less than they should be in everyday life. The mind is like a hand, fashioned to seize and mould the outside world into symbols. All too much, the mental process is aimed only at action, for in our time control of the environment has soared in importance, and there is so much pressure to be active and outgoing that the receptive or contemplative functions are downgraded. These functions may eventually, however, prove to be as useful as those geared to direct action if the human race is to develop or even is to survive.

Research has given us many hints as to how the aesthetic experience may originate in the brain. The motor (efferent) and receptor (afferent) nerves are well known, along with the sensory cortex, electric currents, pattern-making and the process of conditioning, or association. Rhythms of brain activity have been investigated and some guesses made as to their relation to image-forming. As far back as 1943 it was shown:

> "that individuals with persistent alpha rhythms which are hard to block with mental effort tend to auditory, kinaesthetic, or tactile perceptions rather than visual imagery. . . .
> A third group (M Type) was further definable as those people in whose EEG's no significant alpha rhythms are found even when taken with the eyes shut and the mind idle . . . and consists of persons whose thinking processes are conducted almost entirely in terms of visual imagery."[1]

[1] W. Grey Walter, *The Living Brain* (Penguin Books, 1961), p. 185.

21

In the same interesting survey of brain research, the author, W. Grey Walter, emphasizes that even after 20 years it is still too soon for any certainties to have emerged:

> "We must be cautious about jumping to any such conclusion as that children only learn later to think in visual terms, although this is suggested by the extreme rarity of M Type children. If, as seems likely, imaginative thinking becomes habitual at about the date when alpha rhythms appear, the startling differences between children, and the critical influence of age on the effects of deprivation, may find an explanation in the tardy and variable development of these physiological mechanisms. . . ."[1]

In short, there seems to be an age for developing sense receptors, and if at that age they are not used they are hard to reactivate in later life. The biologist is not completely sure whether brain rhythms are inborn and hereditary, but it seems to have been established, again according to Mr. Walter, that *it is in the periods when rhythmic activity is minimal that we should expect the closest correspondence with mental states.*[2] This has direct bearing on the nature of the aesthetic experience. The suppression of the normal action-oriented mental processes is essential to the true reception of art. It seems that we have the nerve equipment ready for the achievement of this "mental state" in which images and patterns can be

[1] *Ibid.,* p. 188.
[2] *Ibid.*

22

fully absorbed. In a lecture on "Brains as Machines," J. Z. Young describes some interesting features of our nerve synapses:

> "Sherrington was able to show that not all of the input has the effect of exciting the cells to carry impulses; some input fibres have the opposite effect of quietening the cells down, of inhibiting them. Each cell, therefore, is influenced by a balance of excitatory and inhibitory states; whether it sends impulses to its muscles depends on which influence predominates."[1]

It remains for biologists, perhaps in collaboration with psychologists, to probe further the physical equipment of the human consciousness. The artistic process, both creative and receptive, may remain as one of the mysteries of evolution. But there is no doubt that the equipment exists and that we take pleasure when it is used. It has surely, like other mental and emotional faculties — and it is a combination of the two — been built up in men over the long past, and carried through the germ plasm in varying degrees and strengths. It might be described as accumulated levels of sensibility.

Great art, itself composed from these depths, calls upon our submerged receptive equipment, plays upon the three levels of our nerve growth. There takes place then a stretching of our faculties of feeling and imagining. The pattern-making, the sensuous, the conceptual-associative

[1] J. Z. Young, *Doubt and Certainty in Science* (Oxford Univ. Press, 1960), p. 48.

23

powers, blended in the mind, willingly submit to the power of the artist's construction, which takes over and directs the reaction. The reward is the pleasure of stretching and exercising faculties — the joy of toning up perception, freshening emotion. Whoever has been able to see through the imagination of a great painter, or know characters through a great writer understands the world a little differently after that experience with, you might say, more *mind*.

Looking at nature, even at human nature in extremes of pain, joy or grief, is not similarly coercive. Looking at a powerful work of art effects a more profound change in us than nature ever can. When we look at a starving child, for instance, our impulse toward active help immediately assuages the emotion of horror or sadness, the experience is shut off by activity of the motor nerves. Whereas Picasso's waifs of his Blue Period transfix themselves inside us; there is no immediate sympathetic outlet and our deep receptors are involved in a significant experience. The focus of the artist is communicated to the beholder. As Mr. Young writes, from the biological platform:

> "The creative artist is an observer whose brain works in new ways, making it possible for him to convey information to others about matters that were not a subject for communication before. It is by search for means of communication that we sharpen our powers of observation. The discoveries of the artist and scientist are exactly alike in this respect. The advantage of describing these creative activities in objective

24

language is that it tells us more about them and enables us to consider how to improve them."[1]

"Alike in this respect," yes, but what an enormous gap between the objective formula or theory and the emotionally heightened sensuous artifact! It is science that produces a theory of evolution, using the logical area of the brain. It is art that itself represents and stimulates evolution, as it exercises and sensitizes all the layers of the mind, including the unconscious. For while biologists like Walter rightly recognize pattern-making and abstraction as a critical phase in the evolution of the brain "which may be regarded as a functional recapitulation of the organ's growth,"[2] they are at the same time slighting the full range of the mind. Total recapitulation of mental growth must include the living emotional elements, especially the sensuous, which art evokes simultaneously with the pattern-making and abstracting capacities. It is a misconception growing naturally out of scientific emphasis that *brain* stands only for logic and learning. The brain, as proved over and over again in the works of art it spawns, is a sensuous instrument with emotional and spiritual functions, as well as conceptual. The practical value of these nerve cells has not been thoroughly realized.

The inheritance of race memories, the shared unconscious of Jung, is a dubious proposition. But it is safe to say that our mental capacities have been bedded down in us over millennia in actual physical changes in the brain

[1] *Ibid.,* p. 120.
[2] *Ibid.,* p. 218.

25

mechanism. The responses to certain stimuli are carried on in the germ plasm, and can be developed or not in the child. All these inherited capacities combined, changed, recombined, have culminated in the human self-consciousness; they have made both science and art grow; they have made man the ruler of his environment. But the mind is still an incomplete instrument and many more changes — biological additions and modifications — are needed to keep him from destroying himself and to carry him toward the ultimate awareness of reality. For this, mystic contemplation, however much it enriches his understanding of the individual psyche, seems less useful than the exercise in sensibility provided by art in all its mediums.

For the artist possesses a fuller range of imaginative capacities than the rest of mankind, as well as more highly developed sense organs. It is likely that the tools which he fashions for our minds to grasp can slowly make changes in the general run of mankind in the direction of higher sense of pattern, deeper feelings, clearer concepts of reality. The kinesthetic experience in our nerves that art communicates — becoming in the mind an aesthetic experience — may very well effect the physiological brain changes needed for the next evolutionary leap. Art sharpens the entire being. We develop our sight through the finer lens of the artist, our ears through his innovations in sound and rhythm, our language through his new combinations of diction and idea, and our total minds through his three-levelled intuition of reality.

It is significant that the organs of aesthetic perception react most strongly to objects or stimuli at a remove from physical contact. A piece of sculpture involves the tactile sense to some extent, but it is the eye that commands the response. It is as if the receptor needed to take in the image from afar in order to achieve any formal organization. The lower senses can give sharp pleasure, but they seem to have been in the long run blind alleys for mental awareness, useful only in a past stage of our evolution. It was the eye and the ear, vision and language that built up man's consciousness. G. Elliot Smith has an enlightening passage on what he considers a sudden, unexplainable mutation in our sense equipment:

> "The attainment of the realization of space and time and the faculty of recognizing objects by their shape, color, size and texture marked the transformation of the ape into a man. For the ability to appreciate the manifold qualities and the distinctive differences made it biologically useful for him to devise names for things and so initiated the development and use of language, with all language implies in the vastly increased capacity for thinking in symbols of value to himself and intelligible to others.
>
> By the development of this line of argument, the origin of speech can be brought into logical connection with the other factors that are expressed in the expansion of the perietal, prefrontal and temporal cortex.
>
> In the primitive human brain, such as the endocrinal cast of pithecanthropus enables us to picture, there is a very pronounced local expansion of the posterior part of the second temporal convolution. This can have only one meaning — the fact that in the earliest

27

known member of the human family there was a sudden
expansion of the acoustic territory for the appreciation
of some form of speech."[1]

If the invention of speech was accompanied by such a
notable expansion of mental faculties, what might not be
achieved in the development of the brain cells by consistent
exposure to the arts, with all that entails of imaginative
stimulation. The mutation in the hearing area of the brain
of primates went far beyond the needs of the organism
for survival and remains a mystery. But certainly innovation
and communication were involved — the same urges that
propel man toward art.

From language and hearing came symbol, concept, idea.
This was a new capacity, for man alone, and with its
development he began to take the lead over nature. Nature
lost a part of its responsibility for evolution. Man now
shapes his environment; he also shapes objects for his
perception and pleasure and for the exercise of the symbol-
making faculties that did not exist in the primitive animal
world. There can be no doubt about the importance of the
cognitive even in the earliest art forms — the idea of
fertility, the idea of a successful hunt, etc. And as the brain
developed in complexity and sharpness, the artifact too
underwent refinement and complexification. For the organs
of reception, the sensitized cells in the brain demanded for
their fullest pleasure — and perhaps for survival and growth
— the presence of the relatively new ideational element.

[1] G. Elliot Smith, *The Evolution of Man* (Oxford University Press,
1924), p. 152.

28

What additional equipment is in the making in the brain no one can yet say. But we know that the equipment which we already have is toned up and enlarged by the aesthetic exercise. Would it not be intelligent to encourage such a development rather than block it off during the plastic years of childhood? We do this when we activate in education only the logical environment-controlling faculties and virtually exclude training in sensitivity to art forms. J. Z. Young, during a discussion of memory and learning, wrote:

> "It has long been known that nerve cells deprived of their normal source of stimulation fade away and may disappear . . . the converse is also probably true — nerve cells that receive a great deal of stimulation become larger than those receiving less."[1]

Interesting research could be done during autopsies to discover what has happened over a lifetime to the brain cells of those who have been either artists or highly receptive to art. How different from other brains is the brain of a great listener or a great critic? And do the outgoing active nerve cells of the creative artist thicken more or less than the receptor nerve cells? Young says that "the cortical cells do differ greatly in size," whereas in the rest of the body they differ only rather little from the average." This leads to the not implausible hypothesis

> "that the brain becomes actually modified or moulded so that it tends to react in certain ways in preference

[1] Young, *op. cit.*, p. 83.

to others. Hobbs, who recently developed this hypothesis in some detail, expresses it by saying that repeated stimulation by any pattern of excitation sets up a closed system of excitation, which continues for a while and ultimately leaves a trace."[1]

That *closed system of excitation which ultimately leaves a trace* defines very neatly what may occur during the aesthetic experience, and the repeated excitation is, unfortunately, exactly what is lacking in the normal education. We are still being trained with a view to action rather than the sharpening of our perceptive faculties. Success in action and logical objective thinking has for some time (though not always in man's history) been placed above all else. The biological value of art training has been given little consideration in our western culture; the full machinery of human sensibility is seldom exercised.

There are schools where the importance of art is recognized but the whole ethos, and the reward system of our society, keeps the majority of children from participating fully or for any length of time. Some systematic research might be started to discover the average age at which a child's sense of form is ready for stimulation, what age his sense of color, and when he is ready to respond fully to all three elements in a work of art. There may be a closing point when unused receptive faculties atrophy. A child cut off from human kind, for instance, and brought up among animals, can never after a certain age learn to make more than the most primitive sounds, for, as Young

[1] *Ibid.*, p. 86.

30

has told us (see also page 29): "There is evidence that the cells of our brains literally develop and grow bigger with use, and atrophy or waste away with disuse."[1] A change in our educational emphasis would allow thousands to be capable of the aesthetic experience all through their lives, not to speak of the climate that would foster the creative artist himself and make it possible for him to achieve greater works.

It is obvious that social pressure plays as large a part as education in screening out certain sensibilities, especially during the formative years. The result is that creative and receptive faculties — i.e. the actual nerve cells — do not seem to have improved with the sophistication of man. When we look through the recent past for signs of a rising level of artistic performance, we are bound to be disappointed. Man has not enlarged his biological powers sufficiently to outdistance by very much the aesthetic force of the cave drawings of Lascaux, some 20,000 years old. A great style may now and then rise to great heights and there has been an increase in complexity and variety, but it is the generally accepted view of biologists that the last 5,000 years have seen no apparent change in the sensory equipment.

We know what happened to an area of the brain when language began to emerge: the sense of hearing made a great leap in complexity, so far beyond what selective breeding could have produced and so in excess of practical needs that it challenges the theory of slow change through the survival of the fittest. Man seems to have found instinctively a way to keep this surplus area of sensitivity alert; he in-

[1] *Ibid.*, p. 36.

vented music, and this developed the acoustical cells even further. This process which we can only call accidental, a blind unguided meeting of animal and reality, is still mysterious in its ways and effects. But it is entirely possible that human beings can now step up themselves the slow unconscious drive toward producing a more powerful, a more aware nervous system. Julian Huxley, in an essay called "Evolution as a Process," makes this quite clear:

> ". . . the final step of progress which produced man was solely concerned with improvements of the brain and its capacities, physiological and mental.
> The new phase of evolution thus opened up was characterized by a new relation between the organism and its environment. The human type became a microcosm which, through its capacities for awareness, was able to incorporate increasing amounts of the macrocosm into itself, to organize them in new and richer ways, and then with their aid to exert new and more powerful influences on the macrocosm. *And the present situation represents a further highly remarkable point in the development of our planet* — the critical point at which the evolutionary process, as now embodied in man, has for the first time become aware of itself, is studying the laws of its own unfolding, and has a dawning realization of the *possibilities of its future guidance or control. In other words, evolution is on the verge of becoming internalized, conscious, and self-directing.*"[1] *

[1] Edited by Julian Huxley, A. C. Hardy and E. B. Ford, *Evolution as a Process, Nineteen Essays* (Collier Books, 1963), p. 22-23.
* (Italics mine — D. M.)

Modification of the germ plasm, which has taken place slowly over millions of years, can perhaps be hastened, through a combination of scientific logic and aesthetic sensibility. Certainly the time is not far off when our old emphasis on physical struggle for survival will fade in importance. Man's slave, the machine, has made a surplus of goods available and, in western countries at least, scarcity is no longer the enemy; the only problem that remains is the distribution of what can be produced. This means that new permutations of power will absorb the interest of society, and men may possibly, if not probably, set out consciously to raise the general level of the human mind.

The great mutation in the organ of hearing and the invention of music were extraordinary transformations. Realization of this biological mystery opens the door to a species of practical mysticism, to the thought that with even more developed sense organs we may eventually come in touch with some new form of reality. Philosophers and religious men of the East have for a long time sought this through contemplation and quietistic separation of mental and physical functioning. But the expansion of consciousness is far more likely to occur in our culture through constant exercise of the whole sensory equipment rather than through withdrawal and turning in on one point of self alone. Some unusual mystics have been able to discover uncharted areas of the psyche with no outside aid except perhaps for the guidance of a great religious leader. But for most of us, some sort of steady stimulation from other human imaginations, involving the physical, emotional, intellectual responses combined, is needed for our growth and transformation.

To achieve the transcendental, first comes the training of our biologically-founded senses.

This training must be our responsiblity, not nature's. Evolution seems to have set us on a high plateau and left us to our own devices. The environment which was the backdrop for the marvels of past evolution, and which we have so drastically changed, no longer suffices. We must change it further and not as carelessly as in the past. It is here that the artist finds his vital role. For his function is not only to reveal through his works the true and false values of our society. He can also alter the man-made world we spend our days in. A sincere intention on the part of society to use the artist and respect his intuition and sensibility would call forth more ability than has ever been witnessed. Once the contemporary idea that art is mere entertainment or personal therapy is abandoned, and it is considered as generally useful if not essential, there might occur a dedicated surge of work on our environment in which few could miss having a part. This happened when the cathedrals were built. It is not beyond the possibility of a repetition. But it cannot be left to chance.

Nor can work on the inner environment be left to chance. Whatever new religion, purpose, or meaning for existence emerges, as it inevitably must, during the next centuries, it will surely have to do with participation in the further development of the psyche, mind, soul or whatever name consciousness will take on in the future. Scientific logic already suggests changes; and art, representing the highest development of consciousness so far, will surely be even more involved than it has been during past religious surges.

34

Of the many realities man can inhabit, the one he makes out of art sets a goal for our best hopes. It will be a long time before multitudes of men have the sensitivity that we all try to reach for and understand in great music or great poetry. But there are signs that our curiosity and insatiable desire for fuller experience will not let us stay where we are. Man has an unquenchable desire to climb higher. It is his good fortune to have the road partially marked out by the pioneers, the artists. What they make concrete in their artifacts is a reality that exists in our psyches. Great art cannot mislead us. Through it we learn new qualities of matter in form, and expand our sensibilities, and find levels in our minds of which we are not aware. Our future lies in the struggle for comprehension rather than in the struggle for existence. In great art the essential nature of what we deal with in life is clarified. Richard Carrington, a zoologist, anthropologist and geographer as well as a philosopher, illuminates the relationship between science, religion and art in his *A Million Years of Man*:

> "If the totality of man is regarded as evolution becoming conscious of itself, then science can be defined as the technique of thought by which this consciousness is critically ordered. Its role is to describe and classify phenomena as they impinge on the mind, and so far as possible to ascertain the laws that govern them. But when we turn to art and religion we are confronted by much greater difficulties of definition. In their highest form (and by this I mean when they have cast off the shackles of primitive superstition) it seems reasonable to suggest that they give a greater insight into the nature

35

of the universe and of man than can be provided by science. This is not due to any esoteric quality in these techniques of knowing the world, but simply because their domain includes a much wider range of perception. . . . The function of art and religion in human evolution seems to be to provide a key to the additional aspects of phenomena with which science is incompetent to deal. They are not concerned with material objects, nor even the atoms that compose them, but with vision. Thus they are highly subjective, and the direct apprehension of either beauty or goodness is not something that can be communicated from one mind to another by rational means. Artistic and religious experience is, however, so common and so consistent in its manifestations that only an exceptionally rash and foolish scientist would deny that it, too, obeyed certain laws. To those who have had such experience it seems extremely probable that art and religion are the keys to a new level of awareness in human consciousness, even though this cannot be "rationally" described. The world to which they give access has bigger horizons than the world of science but is not at all in conflict with it. It seems to be a natural continuation of the evolutionary sequence that has already led from inorganic matter to the mind of Homo sapiens."[1]

The connection between religion and art is so clear to this philosopher-anthropologist that he seems to abolish definitely the concept of art as a mere tool of religion. Art

[1] Richard Carrington, *A Million Years of Man, The Story of Human Development as a Part of Nature* (New American Library, 1964), p. 264-5.

at its best is both created and received in an experience as strong as the religious revelation and very much akin to it. And as the "shackles of superstition" fall away more and more, the two exercises in comprehension of reality will come even closer to each other. It is possible that a religious movement based on the further perfection of man's consciousness may grow out of the biologically-fruitful aesthetic revelation. For as old religions die, and economic activity fades in importance, this may become the only permanent, shared mystique left in our jaded civilization.

(The author is aware that biologists will generally bridle at the notion that any experience can have a direct effect upon heredity. But they agree often that the future evolution of man will be in the area of social change. To such objections the answer is that art has an obvious deep and comparable effect on society as on the individual. The effects of art are cumulative and it passes on its discoveries and organization of experience with great dependability. So the argument from biology remains pertinent even if the biological effects are limited to the imprint of art on social organization. So we say that through the impact of art man makes for himself a new environment which in time spells an evolution in man's sensibility whether through changes in individuals or in the social organism or both.)

II

THE

USES

OF

PLEASURE

"If the doors of perception were cleansed, everything
would appear to man as it is, infinite.
For man has closed himself up till he sees all things
thro' narrow chinks of his cavern."
  William Blake, The Marriage of Heaven and Hell

Sexual pleasure is our reward for preserving the body
of the race. Aesthetic pleasure might be thought of as our
reward for advancing the human psyche. It is as if nature
had different but parallel processes ensuring physical survival and mental advance. Both involve pleasure; and
Spinoza's notion that pleasure is the passion by which the
mind passes to a higher state of perfection takes on an
added meaning from our knowledge of evolution.

The mind is the cauldron where symbols are grown,
and the creation of symbols is not without its rewards. The
heart of the pleasure we call aesthetic is probably in the
physical change that takes place when receptor cells of
the brain are agitated in the act of receiving the impact of
an art object. The resulting thickening and strengthening

of such centers probably gives rise to further pleasurable sensations. It is as if interior muscles were being trained by the process of seeing and hearing. The aesthetic athlete enjoys a painting or a piece of music because his nerve centers are being toned up to a new and challenging degree. All the accumulated powers of his brain stem, both its most ancient and recently acquired, are alerted and distended by the intrusion of a work of art that has been made by a human being, expressly designed to impress the receptor nerves of another human being into sharper attention than usual. Our athlete rejoices in the mental sensations of increased awareness, firmer responses, finer feeling.

Though the aesthetic pleasure never matches the sexual in intensity, it can be increased with use. Its varieties are manifold. The aesthetic orgasm involves sensitivities that many people hardly know exist. All too often they are repressed from an early age. This is especially so in our society where the money rewards for most people come from the use of logical or muscular faculties. Ordinarily there is little monetary gain from the exercise of our full receptive powers — including our sense of form and color. Indeed, if one wants to ridicule a man, let him be shown as *Time* showed Nehru (in a photograph that accompanied an antagonistic article) contemplating a flower. More rugged performances are demanded of the male animal, and it is necessary for him to leave some of his sensitivities unused, or even to destroy them, in order to keep the respect of our American society.

But is it living fully to suppress whole areas of our

physical equipment? Why does so much of the effort in education go into teaching logical useful thinking and so little into developing the complex machinery of reception? In our day aesthetic faculties are usually suspect; public opinion and economic fears shut us off from a whole area of learning and enjoyment. Like birds separated from the flock when very young, who do not learn the songs of their species, we lose the nerve cells that could respond more deeply to forms and colors and sounds.

Aesthetic pleasure known during youth prepares the way for the fuller experience. The analogy with the sex act may be somewhat forced, but it is revealing. If one thinks of the supreme joy that art can give as enriching our individual sensibilities and in the long run enriching the whole race, some elements of the comparison fall into place. Form then becomes the virile element with power to penetrate into the accumulated past which we carry inside us. Alone it leaves no fructifying deposit. The sensuous living element is quickening and reassuring at once. And the conceptual content, the nucleus of meaning, is the fertilizing element, creating new concepts and realizations.

Without the vital germ of meaning, a kind of sterility occurs: the entire brain stem is not stirred to creation. Yet an excess of ideational content, not thoroughly absorbed into form, is by analogy another kind of impotence, ejaculatio precox. Without adequate stiffening through form, there can be no entry into the psyche's depths. The great work of art contains stimulation on all three levels. Our receptive powers have come a long and complicated way, and the free use of any one of them has a bit of the aesthetic about it that some time in the past may have been of use in furthering awareness — senses of smell, taste, touch, and temperature reaction. But none of these, nor any other receptive faculty, taken singly, is capable of producing the aesthetic orgasm. It is a complicated experience that must take place on all three levels of our nervous system — the levels of form, feeling, meaning. Any exaggeration, moreover, of one of the elements in a work of art, such as sensuousness, can have a frustrating effect. One thinks here of the surfeits of some of the romantic poets and painters, or the hyper-sweetness of certain music. Overbearing formal qualities can also cause rejection, as in architecture that is so cold as to be frightening in its social implications.

It is obvious that the pleasures of art, however poignant, are less visceral than sexual joys. The word "spiritual" has become jaded, but there is no other term for describing the powerful, cool, transforming effect of great art on its audience. After the experience, we return to our lives with new strength and fresh vision. The curiously heightened contact refreshes our whole biology without demanding anything from us except a voracious receptivity. From Ghirlandaio's portrait of a man and child in the Louvre, you may receive a momentarily complete understanding of the quality and meaning of love such as is rarely experienced in personal life. Few of us can see in a living human face all that is there. Like a landscape, it needs the organizing imagination of the artist. You will find that you recall the self-portrait of Van Gogh in the

44

Jeu de Pau me Museum in Paris more readily than the face of a visitor in the same gallery which you have observed for an equal length of time, and with equal attention. Picasso's starvelings, reinforced by color and line, and shining with his accurate genius, impress us as no actual beggar possibly can. Our receptor mindset is reordered.

Just as the aesthetic pleasure is less visceral it is also far less outgoing. It probably begins in a different area of the brain, in our afferent nerve cells, and is linked with the ancient receptive system of the spinal column. It seems as if after receiving a strong impression, we are able to hold it and let it spread along a line of sensitivity until it stops. There is no outgoing reflex action; our efferent nerves are stilled while at the same time our afferent, receptor nerves are strung up. The pattern-making area of our brain is at work.[1] Also, associations of which we are unaware are revived and we seem to be constructing, with the help of the artifact, something new out of our subconscious stores. The pleasure is that of receiving and conceiving at once. We are linked to the magnet of another human imagination. When intensely felt, a play or painting or poem is hypnotic, freezing all our outgoing impulses and allowing us to have poured into our total awaiting energies what we can only call a revelation.

---

[1] "That we can conceive at all is due to the obscure workings of the brain regions which yield least to experimental probing, the association areas, sometimes called 'silent' because their oracles are dumb when threatened by the experimental intruder. These regions make up the greater part of the human brain and are closely linked with the receiving areas where impulses from the receptors most commonly arrive." Walter, *op. cit.*, p. 71.

Nature too can be said to give aesthetic pleasure. But what is lacking is the magnet of another personality to coerce us into pattern and concept. Nature is living; she has form, rhythm, color (in fact, is the originator of them all) and has emotional associations for us which are undoubtedly inherited from our past. But nature is never complete or finished enough. We are forced to do some rearranging even as we look. What we see in the landscape is unorganized, and the muscular and mental effort we are obliged to provide lowers the aesthetic excitement. This is suggested by the biologist:

> "The proportion of the visual field (of the retina) which can receive a precision image is only about one-hundredth of the whole. . . . So in order to view that landscape which you thought you could take in at a single glance, you have to make several hundred peeps and sweeps, requiring thousands of coordinated eye movements to scan the scene. With the additional effort required for discrimination of colour and third dimensional position, this sounds tiring. And physiologically it is. For the nervous system, looking at a picture of a landscape is vastly easier than looking at the landscape itself. The reproduction of a scene that in nature extends across half our field of vision, reduced in size to subtend a smaller angle, say ten degrees, and flattened and shorn of irrelevant details saves an enormous amount of effort. . . . No doubt the lessening of the strain has something to do with the particular pleasure we feel in looking at a painting or a photograph."[1]

[1] *Ibid.*, p. 77.

This "strain" on our outgoing motor nerves keeps our receptor centers from doing their best work of pure absorbing. Reorganizing and transfixing is the artist's work, and nature is grist for his mill. It is his special pleasure to unify nature's elements according to his superior imagination. If we are lucky, he will not omit from his new construction the germ of meaning.

While psychologists are fascinated by the neuroses of the artist, very little research has been done on the actual physical qualities of his nervous system as compared with non-artists. But it seems safe to say that the artist's outgoing as well as receptive nerve cells must both be highly developed, since he is not only sensibility incarnate but also a man of action in the literal if not the colloquial sense of the words. As René Daumal said, art is "knowledge realized in action." [1] Whatever the balance may be of afferent and efferent nerves in the artist himself, it was probably variation in the evolution of the receptive nervous system — and the pleasures therefrom — that caused the different arts to develop. We know that heredity is a factor of artistic talent and that sensibility is a genetic as well as an acquired trait. It is not too fantastic to assume that certain cultures have produced generations of audiences as well as artists more highly perceptive along some lines than others. Even now some modern nations seem more visual, some literary, some more musical. The spread of peoples and of art works has distributed widely both talents and habits of reception, but there remain enormous

[1] *Mount Analogue* (Pantheon Books, 1960), p. 152.

individual differences in the level of reception achieved. Those ready to receive form will rejoice in Mondrian or Poussin, and will be especially drawn to architecture. Others, leaning toward the sensuous, will revel in Bonnard, in Keats. Still more, seeking primarily meaningful human emotion, will react profoundly to Giotto, Rembrandt, Beethoven. There is a great gap in aesthetic flexibility between the man who can enjoy only the secure and formal music of the 15th to 17th centuries and the listener who is willing to take to himself the chaos, diversification and anguish of a Varese, a Stravinsky.

Of all the different arts, music is paradoxically the most physical and the most esoteric at once. Its uses and pleasures (often so poignant as to approach pain) range from the primitive to the ineffable. We are tuned up by music and vibrate at the ear drum as if we were ourselves instruments. Through rhythm, the formal and sensuous elements become intensely coercive, and the rise and fall of sound, occurring in the dimension of time, more clearly parallels the sex experience than any other art. In music our emotions are directly shaken and changed to a degree that painting cannot match.

The physiological difference between hearing and sight is significant here. Instead of forming a model, in the brain, of the outside world, which is what happens when we see, when we hear we receive mathematical patterns of sound which play upon and sensitize an inner sounding board. Probably through environment as well as through the inherited germ plasm, those who are musical have an innate sense of "rightness" with regard to these patterns, and their aesthetic pleasure in music is to a degree recognition. But tonal systems of "rightness" differ so widely among cultures that it is often difficult for the great music of one racial group to find true aesthetic reception in another. The plastic shapes and the reference to the outside world which allow painting and sculpture for instance to spread their pleasures throughout the world are not present in music, even if you consider a tonal system a shape, and an element of form. Fine music is not *understood* as easily as is outstanding work in the plastic or literary arts; comprehension of the pattern is a more esoteric and complicated process.

On the other hand, on the deep level of rhythm, music is the most primitive and universal art. The area of the brain that receives the pulse of sound may have been developed earlier than the area for sight. There is more direct physicality when the ear drum vibrates than when the eye cones accommodate to color and shape. The distance is less from the ear to the inner hearing center, and there seems to be less brain mediation. Hearing is a less cool sense than sight; the assault on the emotions is warm and sharp. Our response to rhythm and interval is strong and inevitable, perhaps harking back to the movement that we know through modern physics is going on within the most solid forms, the nearest thing to primal energy man has been able to discover. As the Hon. J. C. Smuts pointed out in his book *Holism and Evolution* in 1926, in a discussion of the new concept of matter:

> "It is these quanta of radiation, released when the electron jumps to a narrower orbit in the atom, that

49

account for the light which comes from the sun and the stars, and in fact all radiant bodies; and it is the definite quanta of radiation so emitted which account for the peculiar spectrum of the elements in the spectroscope. Why atomic light should be emitted in these definite amounts of quanta is not yet known, but it is known that the quanta follow a scale somewhat similar to the notes in music, and we may therefore think of light as the music of the spheres, in which the total harmony or light effect is made up of definite discontinuous notes instead of continuous variations of light."[1]

The power of music over us in this primal sense may always remain mysterious. The composer superimposes his individual message through his use of the mathematical scale, and the sensuous colors of the various instruments. Comprehension of this message is easy for some, and for others vague and evanescent, depending on the quality of their sense organs and the training they have had in the early years. Yet even when only dimly comprehended, and bearing no significance for us vis à vis the external world, music can give us a more intensely felt pleasure than any other art. The construction of music is such a remarkable product of the human imagination and so divorced from the nature we normally witness that one must feel that here art is in its own terms approaching some of the mathematical-physical truths of the universe. And with these truths our biologies, however unconsciously, line up.

[1] Hon. J. C. Smuts, *Holism and Evolution* (Macmillan, 1926), p. 40.

In his chapter on "Mechanism and Holism" Mr. Smuts provides yet another clue to the mystery of music's power:

> "Life is a new structure of the physico-chemical structures of nature. . . . There is an element of newness, of structural and functional newness, introduced, but the new does not conceal or annul the old . . . the one is a continuation of the other . . . not a denial of and a going back on the other.
> Thus life is a structure like matter; and a structure in a similar state of unstable equilibrium. The change of equilibrium has the same rhythmic character; only this character is far more noticeable and pervasive than the similar phenomenon in matter. The rhythmic oscillation becomes the distinguishing mark of the functions of life-structures. The pulsations, the rhythmic flow of the functions of cells form the law of life, and incidentally become the basis of the new element of music in life; they give to music that primordial fundamental character which takes us back to the very beginnings of life on this globe . . . The rhythm of equilibrium shows the close linkage between the physical structures and the life-structures. And its music links all life together through all the ages."[1]

Critics, who perforce must use words, those latecomers in our evolution, have a much harder time interpreting music than other arts. A special language has grown up to describe what seems so disassociated from everyday reality. This abstraction, this "purity" is a great strength

[1] *Ibid.,* pp. 175-6.

in music, but it is not a quality that can be carried over whole and idealized in the graphic or literary arts. The latter appeal to different areas of our nervous system and create different pleasures. They have different biological origins. Aesthetics viewed biologically thus is freed from the old incubus of trying to prove that all art comes under one rubric. Painters might consider whether crossing the arts is not likely to breed weaker hybrids. Painting which seeks in extreme ways to imitate music leaves out the levels of human meaning it should include, without at the same time reaching the rhythmic emotional depths of musical performance. Musical painting is a mirage. The inner world, that deep rhythmic oscillation in which our cells as well as the stars partake, is an entirely different medium from the outer more solid, more individuated world that painting can digest — and does, when not driven from its function by social distortions.

The impact of painting must therefore be far less physically moving, and far less esoteric than that of music. Compared to the use of geometric form in painting, musical form is fluid and molten, disembodied energy, with an effect more fleeting than that of an object made out of earth solids (which of course are not truly solid) and modelled after images of ourselves. It is one of the triumphs of the psyche that we can receive from the composer, even in such an abstract medium, his messages of joy, sadness, courage, grief. The mutation of the human hearing cells has already been mentioned as a great mutation. The invention of music, like mathematics, seems to have been aimed at eventual comprehension of a still unknown area of reality.

Mathematics and physics exercise the cognitive level of our brains, and are disciplines that only a few can enjoy. Great music with its total biological pull can take any human being at least part of the way into another chamber of consciousness. It is an exercise in reception that must inevitably have evolutionary significance.

Though belonging to literature, poetry is an art akin to music, based on rhythmic form, and using vowel and consonant tones for color and texture much as music uses the different instruments. It is of course, like all the verbal arts, so compounded of meaning that this exclusively human element far outweighs the formal and the sensuous. A word *is* a meaning, and can never be rightly employed for its sensuous quality alone, or abstractly, without reference to human associations. Literature emanates from the most recently-grown portion of our nervous system, the cognitive area that invented first speech and then writing, and it demands primarily our comprehension of ideas and values. Yet the sensuous-emotional and formal elements are very important — great writing is never without them.

More than any other form of literature, poetry strikes at the sense organs that also respond to music and evokes the same deep pleasurable recognition of movement in time on an ordered scale of intervals. Pattern is essential to a poem, as well as anticipation, rise and fall, resolution. Koestler, in his *The Act of Creation* writes:

> "Rhythm and rhyme, assonance and pun are not artificial creations, but vestigial echoes of primitive phases in the development of language, and of the even

more primitive phases in the development of living matter; hence our particular receptiveness for messages which arrive in a rhythmic pattern, and their hypnotic effect. Association by sound affinity is still employed in unconscious mentation; it is manifested in the punning mania of children, in sleep, fatigue and mental disorder. The poet creates by bisociating sound and sense, metre and meaning; his voice is bi-vocal — so to speak."[1]

To metre and meaning one must add the third ingredient — physicality, the sensuous color of the visual imagery, which Koestler describes as "derived from the most important sense organ" and carrying a special appeal to our emotions:

". . . the 'picture-strip' language of concrete imagery pre-dates conceptualized thought. The highest emotive potential is found in images which evoke archetypal symbols and arouse unconscious resonances. They lead to the 'earthing' of emotion by relating particular experiences to a universal frame, the temporal to the external. . . ."[2]

What do our sensibilities gain from that rarest artifact, the great poem, beyond the arousing of "archetypal symbols" and "unconscious resonances?" Truth and beauty have been the stock phrases; more specifically, a psychic intimacy is set up between the poet and his audience — we are aroused to participate in his unique transcendence

[1] Arthur Koestler, *The Act of Creation* (Macmillan, 1964), p. 343.
[2] *Ibid.*, p. 343-4.

54

of verbal material. His logical ordering of his insight into reality moves us as much as his music. He is making a complex construction of words on which we can test ourselves over and over again.

The poetry in Shakespearian plays — the combination of sensuosity, wisdom, and the rhythm of the pentameter handled with genius — is one reason why the plays survived long after the plots and staging became outmoded. The other reason of course is the creation of characters that seem to have a permanent life in the midst of the illusion they inhabit. A play is the literary form that illustrates most clearly the three levels of art: the stringent form held in by time and stage; the living sensuous characters speaking words that in the greatest plays have the heightened quality of poetry, against the color and texture of the set; and last, but most, the theme or meaning of the drama — essential if it is to affect our total sensibility.

The language of the novel is less heightened, but this newer art form has a special place in our present civilization and a value all its own. Less formal, closer to the rhythms of everyday conversation, the novel at its most effective forms a pattern in the mind of the reader through which he later looks out at the world, a world that is never quite the same, for example, after reading Proust or Turgeniev. Drama also can change our point of reference but the impact is more condensed and pointed; the catharsis of our emotions is all-important. The imprint of the novel builds up slowly, and is less physical, more like the reception of painting than music. Through the novel we can stretch

55

our consciousness tenuously but permanently, and see human possibilities and qualities we would never have guessed at. Socially and psychologically analytical, the novel is the logical product of a self-conscious civilization, at the farthest remove from the climactic rhythmic arts of music and drama. Its forerunner was the long narrative poem; it tells the story of the trials and adventures of the psyche in its journey through society as Homer told of the physical and moral trials of Ulysses.

Trillions of words have been written about language; the destructive or constructive effects of words, moreover, is well known in this time of excessive printing and swift communication. But, as Herbert Read says, "there are two competing systems of communication, one based on *sound,* the other on *sight* . . . the system based on sight has been underrated and sadly neglected by modern society, and . . . any satisfactory social integration of personal intelligence requires the full development of both systems of communication." [1] The graphic and plastic arts have more power over us than we realize. Every day even the untrained eye is receiving in town or city adumbrations from the art of the past. Greek, Roman, Renaissance motifs permeate all our buildings, public or private, except those made during the last decade or so. Our moods and even our behavior are subtly influenced by use of space, decoration — by the ambience of order or that of chaotic ugliness. Our reactions, however implicit and undeveloped, never

[1] Herbert Read, *The Forms of Things Unknown* (Horizon Press, 1960), p. 34.

56

stop. More explicit, stronger reactions could proceed from the training of our visual tools; the results would be a more congenial and productive environment which science alone can never achieve.

Architecture, more material, less animate than the other arts, is ruled by the formal element: Read calls it the "apparently infinite series of variations on a relatively few fixed forms." [1] For however much function or utilitarian meaning wedges its way into the design, or texture and decoration add their sensuosity, the appeal is, like that of sculpture, primarily to our senses of volume, space, equilibrium. Long before we know that architecture exists, we live in a world of weights and balances, horizontals, cubes. The nerves that deal with these realities get stronger as we test them against nature and later against man-made constructions which are more demanding and coerce us into patterns. It is interesting that Mondrian, defining abstract painting, should provide an accurate view of the architectural process:

> "When dynamic movement is established through contrasts of oppositions of the expressive means, relationship becomes the chief preoccupation of the artist who is seeking to create equilibrium. . . .
> Intrinsic reality — dynamic movement — is established in abstract art by the exact determination of the structure of forms and space, in other terms through the composition."[2]

[1] *Ibid.*, p. 59.
[2] Pieter Mondrian, *Plastic Art and Pure Plastic Art* (Wittenborn, 1945).

Participation in an architect's "organization of space," however, cannot help but be a deeper emotional experience than feeling and comprehending the structural composition of an abstract painting. Meanings, which can only be said to be on the human level — dignity, grandeur, significance — grow out of the forms and out of their palpability. To be within the Pantheon in Rome, for instance, is to feel quite physically how a single large form broadens our sense of being enclosed in a perfectly balanced construction. Even though it dwarfs a human being in size, yet it gives him a feeling of magnificence and power. There is a sensation of swimming or floating through a meaningful, almost tangible, pool of space. The interior of Chartres expresses and evokes another kind of spatial ecstasy. One is enclosed and lifted at the same time, as the structures, especially the columns, pull one upward in a virtual flying. In Mont St. Michel, one is assaulted by a series of enclosed spaces. Massive columns and strong stone arches at the bottom reassure us that we are anchored to the earth. Slowly we climb into an area of lighter, smooth-textured stone and more delicate columns, in a progression that never goes beyond what our sensibilities can absorb.

If form and space were all, the total effect of the cathedrals would be less. But each section of Mont St. Michel, each change in size and tone, has meaning, and speaks to us of the life of the times. At the very top, the delicate columns and the materials describe the significance of the cloister high up on the great rock. Meaning has been articulated through a most profound identification with form. The Pantheon, with its architecture so unlike the

58

Gothic, expresses an entirely different way of living and feeling. We respond to them both, taking pleasure in our own psyches from the imagination that went into the stone — enjoying the power that was able to symbolize the human environment by invading and organizing space with a structure we never could have imagined out of our own experience.

As in modern painting and sculpture, emphasis on the formal abstract element already so strong in any construction that must stand up, and be lived in, has dehumanized architecture to a point that is almost frightening. A boring rather than dynamic repetition of line cuts down to the minimum any aesthetic pleasure in our skyscrapers. The movement that in the earlier part of the century cleared away eclecticism and gave us new perceptions of light and space seems now to be in slavery to engineering. It takes more than technology to produce grandeur. The utility, the money-making power, of a building seems to have crowded out the aesthetic urge, which is to be expected in a society devoted to affluence and scientific experiments. Private building offers a chance for a more human architecture, but here too our economic system discourages the individual, originating aesthetic drive in favor of technological advance. How could it be otherwise until we are trained to see more clearly and understand the forms and linear rhythms that satisfy our total biology?

Sculpture, appealing to a tactile as well as visual sensibility and once wedded to architecture, has gone the way of painting into abstraction. This art, which Herbert Read suggests, started with the "deep-seated longing that man has to project an icon, a material counterpart of his mental image of himself," [1] has nowadays reduced both its sensuosity and its significance by an excessive indulgence in dehumanization. Man's image of himself has slowly shrivelled to a matchstick, and now often disappears entirely into a geometric form, an artifact conceived on only two levels of our creative and receptive faculties — those of texture and rhythmic form. Again one asks oneself, as when faced with abstract painting no matter how expertly conceived, whether the omission of the third level of appeal to the human imagination is likely to enhance the value of the art object or our joy in it. The great sculptures of India, Greece, Rome, Renaissance Europe give witness to what man can feel, and remain as instruments for our exercise and our delight.

Each art form makes its own unique contribution to a separate function of the brain. Pleasure, at the base of the aesthetic experience, is different for each area of nerve involvement, though its purpose remains the same. The parallel lines of sexual and aesthetic communication draw closer together in the art of the dance. Dance is related to sculpture, and like that art expresses ideas through images of the body itself. It goes much further than sculpture, using the body itself instead of inanimate material as the formal element, which is organized by the performer into rhythm and dramatic meaning. Patterns made and quickly unmade pass before our eyes. As in music, which the dance uses to complete itself, the meaning as well as the form

[1] Read, *op. cit.*

60

has an evanescent quality, even when a story is being told. Yet when behind the performer there is a great choreographer, manipulating both design and emotional significance at the beckoning of fine music, then all parts including the sexual become blended into a work of art that is solid and fluid at once. Great dancing attacks several areas of our psyche and while it can be exceedingly earthbound, it can also rise to extraordinary heights of human communication.

As an even more inclusive combination of the arts, and one peculiar to our time, the motion picture has emerged as the first mass art capable of touching all sensibilities, a universal medium that could indeed effect changes in the long run in the human consciousness. It is nonsense to complain about the "mass society" and the mediocrity that is supposed to result from universal literacy and education. This point of view, fundamentally feudal and archaic, fails to take into account the biological value, nay necessity, of including everyone, all human classes and potentialities in the furthering of our evolution. During our history, each changing social system, from slavery through feudalism and capitalism and now into socialism, as it became possible for more people to enter into the benefits of the society, has invented new art forms that would reach those people. From minnesingers who recited poetry to the court we came slowly to the invention of printing, to the elaboration of printing, to the novel which can reach millions. From private purchase of painting and sculpture we have come to the greatly improved color reproduction. Finally, photography and a dedicated scientific age have brought us the motion picture. This is a progression for which we should be grateful, even if the cinema and TV are still in an unsophisticated stage, like the early simplified novels.

The novel is for the many; the motion picture is for all. It travels readily through all cultures, and it operates full force on all three biological levels of our reception — a natural vehicle for furthering our sensibilities if we should decide to go to work at it. Unlike opera, in which sound, sight and meaning are rarely if ever fused successfully, the cinema by its very nature is able to blend many arts into a unified expression. The appeal to the eye and ear is simultaneous; an artist working in this volatile very human medium can combine design, sculpture, dance, literature, drama and music. This can be experienced in the brain as a unity, a fused response in the nerve cells. The full potential of this new art is yet to be achieved; few films come up to the standards already set by the other arts. Money values still repress creativity in the cinema as they do in the theatre, and aesthetic purpose is too often thwarted.

This is not to say we have not had great films. For the most part they have stressed meaning rather than form, as in the Russian movies produced in the free early days after the revolution. Italy, when fascism was ended, put out a series of fine documentaries, and America too has done some sensitive social films. And the great acting performance of an artist like Chaplin, permanently preserved on film, makes us realize what the medium can be made to do for us.

Chaplin was an innovator and in a sense created his own medium. His work was a prophecy of even more disturbing "modern times" to come. It may need a transformation of society to inspire artists to dedicate themselves as he did to full expression of human and social realities. Until the world is more acceptable and less terrifying to the artist, and has a new set of values we shall have to content ourselves with the products of his alienation and his fear. Because of the economics of movie making and the ruling power of business over the film industry, the artist has a small role in the cinema today. But it is a new art, and gives some pleasure merely by existing at all, and by its implicit potentiality as the most powerful instrument of symbol-making ever known.

The aesthetic pleasure comes when we keep our outgoing motor nerves dormant and use to the full pitch of intensity our receptive powers. These powers exist in all of us in varying degrees and in varying sense organs. The pleasure appears to be our guarantee of nature's will to increase our sensibilities and prevent the atrophy of the senses that have already developed in such complicated ways. It would be a cruel deprivation to let brain cells decline through lack of use. If they are kept lively and growing, we have a never ending source of delight. Man lost his once sharper sense of smell as he rose to his feet and found sight and hearing more effective working instruments. What was lost opened up other areas. Further enrichment and enhancement wait only for a concerted attack by men who not only believe in evolution, but also believe that it can be consciously and deliberately quickened through the pleasurable use of the aesthetic imagination.

III

A
NEW LOOK
AT
ART THEORY

CHAPTER THREE

The biological focus can shed some light on art theory and criticism and on the requisites of a good critic. For if one considers a few of the philosophies of art, past and present, one finds imbalances that can be attributed as much to the biological as to the intellectual traits of the critics and historians involved.

Unlike the artist, who can operate brilliantly even when working on only two creative levels, the critic needs an unfailing three-fold receptivity. He must react equally to pure form, to sensuosity, and to ideas. The development of this biological equipment is the only way that he can perform with any greatness his function, which is to keep the past alive but at the same time understand the art of his own period when it breaks away from old forms. Good critics are rarer than good artists, because so much more is demanded of them in terms of intuition and flexibility of response. The critic's mental equipment must be more balanced. He must react to the most primitive and the most sophisticated art with equal interest and an almost childlike willingness. He must be able to give up prejudice

67

and see beyond the modes to which his knowledge and
memories and modern society in general have conditioned
him. Above all, perfection of taste requires in a critic an
experienced, well-exercised nerve reception to any combination of the aesthetic elements in a work — from the most
abstract of abstractions to the fullest realism — plus the
intellect to evaluate what the artist is trying to say and
how effectively he is saying it.

The artist can be less balanced than the critic and still
be effective. Though the greatest art tends to wholeness,
this does not mean that an artist cannot be weak in one of
the three elements and still great. Poussin, for instance,
was high in form and low in color; Dreiser and O'Neill
were weak on the sensuous levels of language; Mondrian
and Pollock excelled on two levels only. The artist, not an
analyst but a synthesist, is free to put forward his own
biological partialities, and to create according to the love
or hostility he feels towards his life and his own era. We
expect the critic, however, to appraise and be sensitive to
many varying personalities and cultures, for only in such
a context can he be a fair judge.

Unfortunately the seasoned aesthetician tends to become
inflexible and confined to a limited range of perception.
He is apt to lean either toward form and sensuosity or
toward the idea content, or at least become so acclimated
to a certain proportion of each in a certain relationship
that we can seldom depend on him when a sharp new
change in technique, or exploration into a new plane
challenges an old trend. The passage of time is therefore
needed for the final, permanent evaluation. The filtering

process is slowly accomplished by the few critics with a sense for all three elements, and who support unceasingly what is valuable while the ephemeral and second-rate slowly sink away.

This lag becomes most drastic when a society and its art separate. Then the artist must struggle most and wait longest for recognition. A novelist like Henry Roth, for example, can have a thirty-year wait. In a time of chaos and transition, hostility is rampant, taste is unsure, and there is a paucity of great critics as well as of great artists. At such a time fads abound, fortified by theories and pushed by critics. The past has seen many theories about art — art as function, as experience, as virtue, as pure "beauty." It is interesting to consider some of them in relation to modern scientific humanism, and the biological significance of art in man's evolution.

One of the prevailing theories equates art with play. This definition, which goes back to Schiller and Lange, seems to us to be false to the point of damage. For the aesthetic experience has a deep and serious purpose with regard to the psyche. Play is by definition transitory and rather meaningless, and indeed the opposite of art. It uses our outgoing faculties; when efferent muscles and nerves, either physical or intellectual, are performing on the outside environment, as in a game of tennis or even chess, we are at farthest remove from the contemplation, the inner tightening of consciousness that is at the heart of the aesthetic ritual. To clarify this distinction should definitely eliminate the play theory which after two hundred years of false credibility still retains some status in texts on art.

69

There are reasons, of course, for this survival. The theory is temptingly plausible. Both art and play are pleasurable, exercise faculties, are luxuries, and appear on the surface to be unrelated to the pressures of economic life. What theoreticians have failed to notice is that they represent opposite forms of pleasure and exercise opposite faculties, and that art has purposes far beyond diversion, relaxation, time passing. Play is all action; art is receptual, non-active, and profound rather than light, preserving rather than dissipating. Play is release from the work of the world; art takes us out of the world into a different dimension of work. Play is play; art is work.

Another notion, coming down to us through Theodor Lipps and Vernon Lee, is that we experience through empathy (*Einfühling*), that we internally mimic, for instance, the rise and fall of the line of a mountain in a painting. It is certainly true that some sort of physical involvement occurs, but it is not as outgoing and muscular as the theory of empathy implies. When one looks at a painting, one may bring to the surface of one's attention the parts of the psyche that respond to what is being presented. But the active participation of bodily sensations — muscular identification — is an absurd concept when applied to art. What the artist sets up in us is more like an internal wrestling match, non-muscular, involving deep-seated nerve tissue. We do not go out into the picture; it comes to us.

Edward Bullogh's exposition of "psychical distance" is much more sympathetic. His idea that when we receive art we put ourselves out of gear with ordinary living

70

corresponds with our biological interpretation of aesthetic energy as something quite free from motor activity. As the practical outgoing reactions are inhibited, and the internal suffusion of energy is elaborated, a process of detachment is set up, which varies with the force of the art object and the discipline of the viewer. To get close to a work of art without losing the sense of distance makes for the ideal reception. One should have the fullest possible involvement in a piece of music for instance, with a minimum of associative thought or feeling occurring to the conscious mind, if the music is to reach at all deeply to the inner sense organs.

Passing from experiential to purely aesthetic theories, one finds how completely the concepts of "beauty" and "ugliness" have been abandoned. One can sit through a whole course in aesthetics without hearing them mentioned once. The old idea of beauty in the sense of something smooth or pretty has been discarded. Ugliness or charm of subject matter is now irrelevant — the emphasis is on effective expression. It is true that ugliness still exists: an object with neither formal nor sensuous effectiveness and with at the same time no significant meaning content, is an ugly object. Artistry is lacking on every level. But if the first two levels of dynamic and sensuous form are effective, no work can be called ugly no matter what brutality or horror is represented, provided one can tolerate the presentation. Goya fascinates us with subjects that would in real life be recoiled from as ugly, and we are not hurt but enlarged by such experience. The notion of the three-tiered response clarifies one of the old paradoxes of art — how could the ugly be beautiful?

Another idea, that art is imitation of reality, has also gone out of date after a long life reaching back to Aristotle. It was the camera that dealt the final blow to precise rendering of the outside world. As perfection of reproduction is approached, aesthetic excitement disappears. What lends interest and tension to a work is the distortion of reality through the artist's vision; also, as Gombrich puts it, we are most pleased when forced to collaborate:

> "Leonardo achieved his greatest triumphs of life-like expression by blurring precisely the features in which the expression resides, thus compelling us to complete the act of creation. Rembrandt could dare to leave the eyes of his moving portraits in the shade because we are thus stimulated to supplement them."[1]

And treating a more modern period, when the large revolt from representational painting began:

> "This Renoir . . . reminds us of the blurring achieved by Impressionism which demands the well-known trained response — you are expected to step back and to see the dabs and patches fall into their place. And then Cézanne with whom activity is stimulated to even greater efforts, as we are called upon to repeat the artist's strivings to reconcile the demands of representation with obedience to an overriding pattern. It is just because this reconciliation is never complete . . . that to us Cézanne can never be boring."[2]

[1] E. H. Gombrich, *Meditations on a Hobby Horse and Other Essays on the Theory of Art* (Phaidon Press, 1963), p. 10.
[2] *Ibid.*, p. 41.

Some defense of realism, however, is in order today, with abstraction more or less dominating the field. The inclusion of some elements of reality, however transmuted, helps to arouse the area of the mind where life experiences are evaluated, stored into memories, later recalled. Abstract art leaves some of this area untouched. Moreover, its refusal to delineate the human has an impoverishing, near-puritanical effect. Certainly the effort to parallel nature exactly has been wisely dropped. But if one feels that a sense of springing joyousness is better conveyed by a dancer's twisting body than by a non-objective set of forms and colors, and is more moving to the beholder, then one cannot help but prefer some rhythmic arrangement of objective reality to the "action" painting of today. The abstractionists seem to have robbed both themselves and us of an important tool, an enriching element of art. The extremity and duration of this impoverishment can only be blamed on our society. In a more secure world, imitation — in the sense of inclusion of elements from the outside world we inhabit — will inevitably return.

There are of course other than social reasons for the rise of abstractionism. It occurred as a posture of art in its own history — a reaction among artists against the weakening of form by the Impressionists. After the turning point of Cézanne came the Cubist surge before World War I. The drive toward the fullest exploration of a new technique or idea is always a factor in the history of a style. The reduction of the amount of representation in a painting, once it started, had to continue until all the possibilities were exhausted. But along with this tide of experimentation there has been since the early days of the century an increasingly menacing social and political climate — a wind that has driven the artists more and more into themselves. Alienated and hostile, they have not been willing to absorb and give back in their work any realistic interpretation of a world which they find so antipathetic. This hostility has been more obvious in literature, especially the novel, which by its very nature must take its material as much from the objective as the subjective world. Abstract writing, as in recent French novels, has so far reached a very small audience.

One cannot underrate the influence of the critics who found excitement in the new trend and helped drive it forward, with theories that swelled the emphasis on those older elements of art — geometric form, sensuosity of line and color — to the detriment of meaning and human significance. They embellished with logic what the artists were doing and created the mystique that is still with us. Clive Bell's *Art* came out in 1913, with the Cubist movement, while Roger Fry was busy against much opposition bringing Cézanne to the attention of England.

Bell found the true aesthetic entirely a quality of form, "significant form" as he called it. He thus separated out only one of the ingredients of art, one side of our biology, and made it stand for the whole of the experience. True, he chose the most essential of the three elements. You can virtually eliminate either conceptual meaning or sensuosity and still have a work that gives some pleasure, but you can never eliminate the foundation of form. But it is certainly not the whole story, and Bell, by adding the word *significant* begged the question. This should have acted as a warning against the temptation of treating form as a be-all and end-all. We must assume that his exaggerated position was a result of the crusade he undertook to weaken the status of the over-sensuous Impressionists and to push forward Post-Expressionism.

It is one thing to prefer to exercise the sensibilities primarily on form and sensuosity, but it is another thing to base an aesthetic theory on such a preference. Some arts could not even exist on form alone. And in the graphic and plastic arts, not even the most dynamic combination of form and feeling makes the best construction for the exercise of the human psyche. Symbols and concepts, though comparatively new on earth, are important parts of man's equipment, functions of his life tension. The artist, if he is to be most effective and fructifying, cannot put them aside. Since man carries through heredity a series of evolutionary biological transitions in his brain and spine, his entire nervous apparatus cannot possibly be reached by an art that is not equally complex. Bell's emphasis had a real point, but by excluding too much, he ended up in an unbalanced position.

Like everyone else, a critic is vulnerable to the value judgments of his times. Roger Fry, though not as extreme as Bell, also put excessive emphasis on form, and ended up with the notion of a very special aesthetic emotion, a response to spatial relationships between plastic volumes. While the isolation of this ancient element was useful and marked an advance in aesthetics, it is quite obviously inapplicable in a general way to all the arts, especially

the literary where the representational is intrinsic. Moreover his theory leaves out the human, cognitive element,
which must be fused with the formal and the sensuous if
a work is to endure. The human values in Giotto are still
there for all to see, and though not as old or deeply
primitive as the formal values in his painting, they have
not evaporated with time, they are still essential. Fry's
devotion to the cause of Cézanne and his followers led
him into a new system of aesthetic criteria which one
cannot help feeling was slightly off balance. Any imitation
of reality, ideas, emotional overtones, delineation of the
human were all downgraded in favor of a "purer" treat-
ment. There was a surge of new interest in structure and
design. African sculpture became fashionable. There were
statements that representation "disturbed" the plastic (as
it indeed must!) and Fry went so far as to suggest that the
curve of fate in a tragic drama was the central strength of
the work rather than the emotional intensity of the contents.
Plastic value, he said, was inside and intrinsic; representation was an invader from without that became dated and
disappeared with the passage of time. I. A. Richards
complained that Fry's special aesthetic emotion was a caprice.
Its direction certainly had value for the painters of the day but
brought us ultimately to such a dead-end extreme as Leepa's
diagrams of weights and tensions in the structure of art.

It is interesting to compare the bias of a modern artist
such as Allen Leepa, as developed in his book, (first printed
in 1949), *The Challenge of Modern Art,* with that of a
philosopher such as W. T. Stace in his *The Meaning of
Beauty* (1929).

76

The aesthetician tends to find art's power in the development of concepts; his emphasis is on the fusion of the intellectual and the visual; sensation must be joined with thought:

> "even in the case of ordinary sense-perception, that which alone makes out of private subjective sensation a public objective reality is the submerged or fused conceptual element. . . ."

or further:

> "beauty is the fusion of an intellectual content . . . with a perceptual field, in such manner that the intellectual content and the perceptual field are indistingishable from each other; and in such manner as to constitute the revelation of an aspect of reality."[1]

The modern artist, on the other hand, seems to be writing in another language:

> "Art is based on emotions. . . . Feeling is the final test of what we do and think as appreciators and creators of art. . . . The contemporary expression emphasizes the individual and his inner world. The content created by the modern artist is profound. In eliminating the emphasis on the outward appearance of the natural world, he may now exclusively concentrate on and express his inner world and its forces. . . .
> The type of emotion with which the artist is concerned

[1] W. T. Stace, *The Meaning of Beauty* (Cayme Press, Ltd.: London, 1929), pp. 43 and 34.

and which we shall find fundamental in painting (and sculpture) has been called 'emotion-tension' or 'force' in this book. . . .

The artist expresses intense emotional tension through an equilibrium of the formal elements of his painting . . . one form cannot act upon another to create a stronger force in one direction without equal opposition somewhere in the picture, for the force is the product of the mutual action on each other of at least two forms, or two elements."[1]

This is language out of engineering and psychoanalysis. The action painters are concerned with form and feeling — highly subjective individual feeling with little reference to outside reality. Ideas and meanings are as taboo as realism. The appeal to the conceptual, cognitive part of the brain is left out. It is as if painters were seeking to take on the role of composers of music, severing themselves from the images of the world which they and their audience hold in common. With formal and sensuous tools only, the abstractionist has been speaking to us in a personal, cryptic language. No matter how talented he is at reproducing his emotions and sensations, we cannot help but feel vaguely dissatisfied and only half-involved in his work, unless by rare chance we happen to share his psychological frame of reference.

Fry went too far in the direction of making the aesthetic experience unique, semi-mystical and esoteric, and thus

[1] Allen Leepa, *The Challenge of Modern Art* (A. S. Barnes & Co. Inc.: New York; Perpetua Edition, 1961), pp. 244 and 113-4.

78

helped non-objective art on its way to cultism. In sharp contrast, John Dewey brought art and every day life together. He thought of all completed experience as a means of making life more coherent and vivid, and thought that aesthetic perception was merely a sharper use of the same faculties that we use for everything else. Anything thoroughly experienced could be called aesthetic, and there was no need to separate out the functions of the mind as it receives imprints either from an art object or a trip to the market. This theory seems extreme and leaves out the obvious fact that the biological reactions to art and every day life are quite different. For one thing, the art object is received with an inhibition of motor activity. For another, art tightly controls the pattern that is printed on the psyche.

While Bell eliminated the value of meaning and representation, these elements played such a large part in Dewey's interpretation that any work, however low in formal and sensuous qualities, could be for him a source of aesthetic pleasure. He suggested that all living had artistic overtones and considered the conscious idea of art as man's greatest achievement. Neither of these ideas can be questioned. But his further notion that any piece of living, if taken seriously and fully realized, is art in germ, is difficult to accept. To be sure, it is important to bring art back into the center of life. It has been driven out not only by theories that make it snobbishly remote, but also by a society which treats it as something eccentric, even neurotic, whereas it should be valued as intrinsic and vital to our existence. But Dewey was over-reacting to the art

79

for art's sake mystique. You might call the new "Pop" art a caricature of his idea. The joke that began with Duchamp has turned sour. One must in the end make a proper distinction between life activities which are aesthetic and those which are not.

While Dewey rightly says that any perception could develop something of the aesthetic, the emphasis should be in the direction of taking in specially prepared objects because in our activist day the aesthetic element is so small in everyday life. We did have evolution before man intervened with art objects. But this development from contact with natural objects unshaped by man made slow progress. Expanding consciousness now needs the help of man-made artifacts to help the process along.

Tolstoi, like Dewey, derogated the formal element. For him the communication of emotion was the true function of art, and he even went so far as to tell us which emotions are best, namely feelings of human brotherhood. No one would doubt the necessity to communicate emotion in art, but the emphasis on ethics seems to fault Tolstoi's thesis. One is tempted to hurry back to Roger Fry and his notion that since there is no call to action in the art experience, art has no moral responsibility. Art uses emotion to hold and stimulate its audience; and the quality of evil can be just as stimulating as that of goodness. The ethical effect of a work of art is no criterion of its power. In the long run, through indirection, exposure to great art makes for increased sensitivity and awareness of reality — including the evil as well as the good.

If we quarrel with those who insist that form is the heart

of art, and with those who overstress the emotional or meaningful, it is because we feel that art's biological role, its evolutionary purpose is to involve the whole man, either as creator or participant. The critic who is a whole man, tuned in through all levels of his nervous system, with no quirks or blocks, no shackles on his emotional responses — that man is the great critic, with an important role interpreting art for his society. The critics of our time seem to have become too intimately involved in certain schools of art. They are often, like the artists, so involved in the two-leveled, decorative style of the day that they cease looking for the profundity, the generalized human insight that marks great work. Color, line, shape, dynamic equilibrium — these are tools, and it is with these tools that modern painters are covering their canvases. The critic learns to separate the good from the poor use of tools; gradually he becomes interested only in these techniques; he develops criteria for successful and unsuccessful abstract art. Some of it appeals directly to his own psychological references. Finally he comes to believe that the good work which he has learned to select is great work, in spite of the fact that it is neglecting the spirit of man as distinguished from his techniques, and in this way the failure of a whole school to say anything on a universal level passes unnoticed. The yardstick that measures the best of what is current and novel is not able to measure the lack of a whole dimension.

The history of art criticism reveals that few men have been capable of spotting the quality of universality in a work of art that makes it endure and become a classic. Indeed the very idea of individual response to each artist did not exist until the 19th century when in France there was a series of acute critcs beginning with Baudelaire. Yet even he, who swam easily in the two currents — classicism represented by Ingres and romanticism represented by Delacroix — found trouble when Manet came along with a new style. For critics must use words, and become accustomed to certain symbols and concepts, and have a hard time following and judging an innovation after they have developed their own approach to the art they knew in their earlier years. Old habits and language become a block to new impressions.

The nineteenth century was slow to accept change but our century, because of the steady deliquescence of values, has swung in the other direction, seeking forever some salvation in the new. Critics today are accustomed to, even afraid not to, appreciate changes. One no longer resents breaches in old habits of perception — on the contrary there is a virtue in acclaiming the evidence of the decay of a unified set of values; each change is eagerly seized and praised. In just a century, beginning with the French exhibitions, we have seen the development of taste in response to each picture and not just to a style, to archaeology and to art history. Yet taste remains a biological mystery and though it can be enlightened it is doubtful whether it can be taught. We have gone from inflexible criticism of anything new to over-eager acceptance of any innovation. The margin of error inevitably grows wider and can only be kept in control by steady vision of the whole contribution from the past. In nineteenth century France, though adventuring among masterpieces began,

82

and for the first time personal evaluations of contemporary works were made by a fine set of critics, yet their experience indicates that time as well as taste is needed for true evaluation.

André Malraux, in his great work *The Voices of Silence,* has summed up the phenomenon of the last hundred years that has made art immeasurably more important to civilization, and its manifestations more stable. The effect of photography — the teaching and spreading through a vast public the art of all ages — means that it is now impossible for taste to be uninformed by the past. It is not probable that an artist will ever again be downgraded for a long period, as Shakespeare was, for instance, before the expansion of printing. Changes in fashion will not outmode painters and a new style will not be able to take over to the complete elimination of the old. The whole pantheon of art will be involved in each change. As T. S. Eliot said, each new work dislocates the whole of past poetry. By the same token, past art, now so available and deeply respected, will indirectly moderate the fads and theories and extreme reactions of the present.

Art at its most effective is as broad and complex as the human mind itself, neither as narrow and bare as modern theory dictates, nor as loosely connected to daily life as Dewey suggested. It cannot be called ethical, immoral, neurotic, therapeutic, recreational or incidental. It is what it uniquely is; and its creation and reception are essential functions of the human biology. One of art's greatest qualities is detachment from the transitory world of action, making its interpretation of phenomena the only reliable record that we have. Men of politics and business, even the historians, seldom see their own time as clearly as the artist can commemorate it in his images. Great art never lies. The prism of aesthetic insight breaks up the world into its true colors, and when the action of a period in history is complete, its reality remains only in the artifacts it leaves behind. The artist's detachment, and his ability to interpret what is happening through his total — conscious, subconscious, sensuous, formalizing — nervous system makes him a carrier of the history of the race. His creations add to the edifice of culture, layer on layer, to be used for our future evolution. Any theory that does not recognize that art to be great must bear some relation, however symbolic, to the vast world of humanity and inhumanity outside of the individual artist and his tools is selling short the artistic profession and the public alike.

IV

THE

ART

CHART

CHAPTER   FOUR

In one of the great banks in Manhattan there is a large
room given over to charts of financial data reflecting
changes in our economy over many years. There are charts
for stock price fluctuations, for interest rate variations, for
movements of gold supply, bond yields and other pertinent
data. The careerings of American business are here clearly
outlined. A good deal of the time the indices, such as the
gross national product, point upward.

Similar charts could be made reflecting the alteration of
our attitudes toward society over the last several hundred
years. These charts would reveal the permanent rather than
the fleeting values of our culture, for the only enduring
record of a civilization lies in the artifacts of the imagination left by the aritsts — not in the charts or graphs of
economic and political power. A culture has many strands,
but its essence, its true significance is seldom grasped by
the power groups that create it. This understanding —
often intuitive rather than logical — is a social function
of the artist.

Artists are not often effectively involved in action nor

are they particularly acute about immediate ideological problems. But they are experts on the condition and the motivations of the human psyche. So while one cannot, at least in our time, look to the artists for specific answers to current questions, yet their words are reproductions of the scene as it affects them. Their opinions may be worthless, but their three-tiered biologic responses are as exact and as dependable as the human mind can be. Their reactions will outlast all other data. Eventually the financial charts now so vivid will lose all importance as social change erodes their relevance to our daily lives. But significant art works never lose their validity — at least not for many centuries. Moreover they are of supreme importance in their own time as signs and symbols of what is to come. A look at the art chart as it reflects, for instance, twentieth century society, is dismaying, and should give us all pause. The curve has pointed for some time distinctly down — indicating persistent disapproval of our culture.

There have been many rises and falls in the production of art. Some arts appear and then vanish. Artists in some periods seem to be normal and healthy human beings; at other times, neurotics are doing most of the work. In our day, perhaps the most relevant trend to chart is still what Oretga y Gasset called the "dehumanization of art." This tendency toward the disappearance of human meaning from art forms has now reached an extreme.

A work of art can be overloaded with current human associations and weakened by it, as in the case of much Victorian painting where an excess of detail robs the work of penetrating power. On the other hand, an exclusive resort to form and color also loses effectiveness. Our bio-logical make-up is crowned by our recently acquired con-ceptual power, and if one accepts the parallel between a work of art and the biological creation that is man, then it follows without doubt that neither an art loaded with meaningful detail nor an art that is completely abstract can be of first rank. The first contains too much of exterior nature; in the second, human nature has been eliminated from the work.

The great variations in the amount of meaning an artist infuses into his work are not essentially his choice; they are imposed upon him by society. This most individual of men is unconsciously but nonetheless vigorously selected and commanded by his environment. The contemporary cultural life around him calls him in or guillotines him into silence, pleases him or disgusts him, and this influences profoundly how much and what aspect of reality or sur-reality he will combine with the formal and sensuous elements of his art.

In an attractive world, where he feels himself a willing part of it, the artist is apt to absorb everything. In an unstable world that lacks unity and acceptable goals, he seems to give up the task of absorbing the world, and takes to his tools and techniques for refuge, referring in his work only minimally to the life he sees around him. The formal and the sensuous take over; the meaningful hides, and communication occurs only at some less complex, more physical level. It is possible that the best work comes when the world is neither too easy nor too difficult to accept, when the artist can create his parables without being too slavishly realistic and crowding his canvas with contemporary cargo, nor yet too unrealistic, that is, rejecting completely the world of human meanings. No art can flourish when the artists find the world totally objectionable. The past thirty-five years seem to have been such a time, and the art chart of this period might well be given some attention by those who control our destinies. The fact that men of power are in our day all too often separated from art by education and training may explain their blindness but does not make them immune to the dangers implicit in the chart.

The artist is in a sense a victim of his times. Each society, through its system of rewards, calls on certain members to portray it. In some periods, like our own, the great men cannot speak at all. Or at times one art, like sculpture, may vanish from a culture that once produced magnificent work. The ebb and flow of meaning in and out of the arts is one thing, but the particular art a people undertakes is another. Some races never produce great music; others produce and stop. It could not be that the ability dies out, or that talent can vary so greatly biologically. There is at most times a prodigious waste of talent. There are doubtless right now many people in law offices, on Wall Street, in laboratories, schools, government agencies who in another time might have become fine artists. Each civilization receives the talent it deserves. Little Athens, with a bare 250,000 people, developed more first-rate artists twenty-five hundred years ago than the United States with its 190 million inhabitants does today.

We live with the notion that going to the office or the

factory is a great virtue. This habit of gainful toil has not always been considered so virtuous. There is a record of a suit for slander brought by a Florentine nobleman in the Renaissance who complained that he had been falsely accused of working — and at painting, too. (How many irate fathers nowadays accuse their artist sons of *not* working!) The esteem we give to the ability to make money, no matter how, may be one of the causes of our poverty of artistic talent. To make a virtue out of action alone is to starve a civilization. The ability to produce goods until there are too many has its fascinations, but the belief that this is the whole of life has led to a rather arrogant blindness to the importance of the artist and to the significance of his clear condemnation of our present society.

The level of a culture can perhaps be evaluated according to the importance it allocates to sensibility. On this scale we would rate low, for though we honor the artifacts of ancient Athens and Renaissance Italy, we do not measure ourselves against these accomplishments nor feel concerned that in art we are comparatively impoverished. Action-oriented America, like Sparta, has paid a high price for its materialistic success. Not only is there a dearth of genius but what art there is emerges as a rejection of the scene. We have gone over the edge of what began as healthy experimentation with the forms of art into a sort of hysterical negation of art itself. Disunity and chaos have taken over the imagination and we seem to be at cross purposes not only with a good part of the globe but also among ourselves. America is suffering a cultural schizophrenia, with an ever-widening gap between men of sensibility and men of commerce. Roger Fry once wrote: "The average business man would be in every way a more admirable, more respected being if his imaginative life were not so squalid and incoherent." [1] This statement is no less relevant after forty-seven years. The situation has, if anything, worsened, as the business world fights to save its aging economic system and preserve a life that has lost its dynamism.

It is interesting to trace on our chart an art form that was originally created and developed by the burgeoning capitalist society itself. It is hard to believe, but the first novelists in the English language were business and professional men who had the imagination and the energy to invent a fresh literary form, the novel, which they used to advance the new system of values and the new society that was then coming to birth.

The first English novelist speculated in tobacco, in hosiery, in shipping. He also manufactured bricks. By the time he was thirty-two he was bankrupt to the tune of $85,000 and at forty-four he crashed again. All his admiration went out to the great merchants, and he tried very hard to become one of them. He married carefully and took care to educate his children so that they could get on in the world. But as he was not just an ordinary businessman, he also entered politics, made a living for a while writing pamphlets, and even spent some time in jail for his politics. Finally, having found no real success as husband, father, businessman or pamphleteer, he tried

[1] Roger Fry, *Vision and Design* (Pelican Books, 1920), p. 28.

something new. At the age of sixty, he wrote a novel. Some call it the first novel in the language — *Robinson Crusoe,* a study in rugged individualism.

Our businessman is Daniel Defoe, and the days are the glorious boom days of eighteenth century England. Defoe did not think of himself as an artist, but as a businessman turned journalist who saw an audience in the rising middle class. To please this expanding reading public, he invented a new product, and was rewarded by great popularity. He repaid society by glorifying in his characters the virtues it loved. Moll Flanders lived by her wits, Crusoe by individual initiative, self-reliance and industry.

Twenty years before Defoe's birth in 1660, the radicals of the day, who were in good part businessmen under Cromwell's leadership, seized control from the king. By 1660, the conservatives had put the king back, but again in 1688 the same group of radicals, somewhat mellowed, gained control. By 1719, the year in which *Robinson Crusoe* was published, society had swung into equilibrium and the center of gravity was the middle class. The first newspaper had been created in answer to the needs of commerce, and the first copyright law had made writing a form of property.

The next British novelist was a businessman too, but a successful one. Samuel Richardson, printer, was born into the middle class in 1689, a year before the merchant radicals' return to power. This power was firmly established by 1740 when Richardson, now retired from business, published his first book, *Pamela.* Pamela was a good trader, and, like *Robinson Crusoe,* her story hymned the virtues

93

of business morality. This novel was also a great success.

Within thirty years after *Robinson Crusoe,* someone from each segment of the middle class world had tried his hand at the novel. Henry Fielding was a lawyer, Tobias Smollett a physician. These writers were not delicate, nor remote from the world around them. Virtually all the novelists of this time participated in and believed in the "solid" middle class precepts and their heroes were often bold young men on the rise. Because the authors were all (except for Defoe) born and raised in the country, they told stories of country living. Yet their values were not feudal; they were geared to the growing mercantile cities. They all belonged to their age and liked it. To be sure, they did not go so far as to create a businessman hero, because this figure was still not quite formed, just emerging into leadership. Pamela was therefore rewarded by a husband from the nobility, because Richardson, while believing in the aspirations of his own group, knew it had not yet reached the highest estate.

By the second half of the century, the novel did not come out so strongly in favor of middle class virtues. The businessmen had made the final climb and were merging with the nobility to become the rulers of England. The spirit of getting ahead had done its work; the wheels of commerce were rolling smoothly. The new push was mostly overseas, as India, Canada and Australia were brought into the empire. By 1776 the ideas put forward in *Robinson Crusoe* were so taken for granted that Adam Smith could crystallize the whole movement of rugged individualism and laissez-faire in his *Wealth of Nations.* The cry for the establishment of the middle class was no longer needed.

The novel of acceptance came out of this era: Sterne and Austen and Goldsmith. These new novelists poked mild fun at the foibles of a materialistic society, but they had no real complaint against it. At the same time, the thriller, the Gothic tale, and the novel of sentiment were born. Walter Scott typifies this period above all others, writing to amuse and inform but not to uplift the middle class reader by showing him his own virtues. At the age of forty-two, he wrote the first of his historical romances, glorifying medieval England and the out-dated mores of the nobility, ignoring the new richesse. He was anxious not to appear to earn his living by the new and not too reputable profession of writing and published his first books anonymously. Even as he openly accepted a title from the Crown, he embarked secretly on a business career in publishing. The interesting point is that he was not in his romances picturing the contemporary scene, nor boosting an ethic useful in the business world. Nothing appears in his books, either, about the factory system. He was glorifying an older period of the England that had by now taken to itself almost one quarter of the globe. Neither Scott nor his audience was interested in affirming the values which had brought such an empire into being. The establishment had been built, and accepted.

Meanwhile England had expanded enormously. The population, fairly stable in the seventeenth century, had doubled in the one hundred years before Waterloo. The large colonial empire had been very important for the growth of the commercial middle class with its expanding trade; along with that expansion, industry began to appear. The eighteenth century saw the growth of many cities, but by the nineteenth the factories were beginning to dominate the scene. With the rise of this industrial complex, the novelist, far from applauding the progress of business as the first group had, and unable like the second group to take the establishment for granted, turned critical. With Dickens, the novel entered its third phase. It is significant that Dickens was only twenty-four when his first book appeared, and that from then on most novelists began to write in their twenties instead of in their forties. Men of sensibility found it harder to participate actively in the business life of this new England in which factory manufacturing, rather than the more adventurous trading was the way to riches. Writers began to turn at a slight angle away from society. Dickens became concerned with the fate of city people and the social problems of the new industrial system. With him, and after him, the middle class lost the novelist. As the factories spread, writers broke up into two groups, neither of which supported business ideology. Those who followed Dickens criticized the social scene; those who followed George Eliot used the novel mainly as a study in individual psychology. The separation from money values slowly widened — through Thackeray, Meredith, Hardy.

Finally, by the end of the nineteenth century, the novel had turned full swing against the middle class. The leading writers of this time, such as Mann, Joyce, Proust, Gide, Dreiser, Lawrence, Huxley, Rolland could not conceivably have been connected with the business ideology. By the early 1900's, novels were consciously depicting a dying social order.

Thomas Mann was only twenty when he wrote *Buddenbrooks,* a three-generation study of a German bourgeois family as it passed from strength to debility and decay. His attitude was unequivocal and there can be no doubt about this condemnation of the middle class way of life by one of the greatest modern novelists. Twenty years later, *The Magic Mountain* appeared, picturing an ailing society symbolized by the tuberculosis sanitarium, filled with characters from all over Europe. Every one of Mann's important novels had a particular physical disease at the core of its plot: *Buddenbrooks:* typhoid; *Dr. Faustus:* syphilis; *Black Swan:* cancer; *Death In Venice:* cholera; and there are more. Both directly and symbolically Mann sang the doom of the class into which he was born.

A completely different but equally great novelist, Joyce, broke with both church and country as well as with the middle class. It is ridiculous to think of him as connected with business, but at one point he tried it. As Herman Gorman wrote: "It was not long before the young Dubliner discovered that Joyce the businessman could not exist simultaneously with Joyce, the artist. One or the other must go. The businessman went." The profound disgust with life that emerges from *Ulysses* can never be forgotten no matter how preoccupied one becomes with his style. For while this novel shows a static world with no hope, yet Joyce (as Richard Ellman's book [1] makes so

[1] Richard Ellman, *James Joyce* (Oxford University Press, 1959).

very clear) though not an activist definitely viewed himself as a socialist. While describing with a brilliant revolutionary technique the cultural and religious breakdown of his time, he was fully aware of the possibility of another kind of society. As two recent Joyce commentators write:

> "In terms of cyclical history, he was able to explain the wasteland atmosphere of his time. The present cycle of the world is fast decaying; it is almost ready to give way to the new era. Its inhabitants are sterile. . . .
> But the new cycle, Joyce felt, would bring good. He waited for this good with patience and resignation born of long disappointment and disillusion: 'Such is manowife's lot of lose and win again. . . . So what are you going to do about it? O dear!' " [1]

Henry James fled America, hoping to find values different from those of his country, and finally resorted to making a world of his own in his novels. In his preface to *The Reverberator,* he writes:

> "and before the American businessman. . . . I was absolutely and irredeemably helpless, with no fibre of my intelligence responding to his mystery."

But of all the talented poets and novelists who created their works in the heat given off by the general destruction of middle class ideals, there was no greater flame than that of Marcel Proust. Social decay was the central theme of

[1] Marvin Magalaner and Richard M. Kain, *Joyce, The Man, The Work, The Reputation* (Collier Books, 1962), pp. 246-7.

98

his work, at the heart of the magnificent *Remembrance of Things Past*. There were two routes, two walks for the young Marcel in the early pages of the novel: one through the middle class — Swann's way; the other the upper class, the Guermantes' way. With amazing prescience and a high inimitable style, Proust shows us the amalgamation and the decline of the two social groups. At the end they are mingled in what seems at first to be a ballroom full of creatures in hideous masks, until slowly it is revealed that we are not seeing masks at all. These are the true faces of the two societies we first saw in their separate splendors and now see united in a terrible corruption and decay.

It is revealing to compare the heroes of the early novel with those created in the late nineteenth and early twentieth century. The assurance and push to "get ahead" in Roderick Random and Tom Jones has turned into the doubts and frustrations of Hans Castorp or Lambert Strether, or the tortured delicacy of perception of a Stephen Dedalus or a Marcel. The hero became the sensitive man, living in a special world, delicate, perhaps sick, but above all imaginative and perceptive, with an astonishing capacity to absorb and understand the world around him. The theme of sensitivity was of great importance to the artist as he turned away from the industrial materialistic world. Retreating to a tower, a mountain, a cork-lined room, he found something he could still sing about — the human imagination, a power he knew of intimately, the only power left for him to love and admire. It was at this time that the greatest began to write for a special minority, and the work became so complex that it was all but impenetrable,

99

as in *Finnegan's Wake*. How different from the simple tales of the early novelists! From easily read works of business and professional men, this relatively new art form developed into the brilliant coruscating displays of complex styles — in effect an end product, the last great fireworks of an emptying world. Beyond the united condemnation implicit in these great novels coming out of Germany, France and the British Isles, no further comment on this level of writing was possible, and there was no hope left for the wise in the society that these giants of fiction pilloried. From then on the quality of the novel has gone down. No greater talent than theirs has appeared in England or in Europe, as wars, depressions and revolutions have followed each other without let-up throughout the still assured but shaken bourgeois world.

The shrinking of the psyche is a subject that cannot produce great works. The talents of Kafka and Beckett have been confined to images of man defeated, man feeble and powerless. In Beckett's "Molloy" man is crawling in the mud, hardly alive, scarcely-breathing, clawing his way to — nowhere. Catastrophe and doom are explicit now, and there could be no sharper comment on the deterioration of the size and spirit of man in the present culture.

If we pick up the chart of the novel in America after the First World War, we can see our writers were not yet seriously involved but still operating under our characteristic native optimism. Their criticism of the business mores of American capitalism was still good-natured. Up to this time, the American novel had followed, slightly behind and in its own original gait, the English novel's ironic

100

comment on middle class ideals. Many American artists had become, like Henry James, expatriates rather than live in what they felt to be a culture inimical to the aesthetic imagination. This habit continued even more extensively after the First World War. The first fascist success, in Mussolini's Italy, following the short abrupt American depression in 1922, did not frighten our writers. They still felt secure enough to jaunt around the world and to write fairly blithely about the corroding effects on the human psyche of the business ethic, and the war and violence it was bound to engender. This era produced a burst of good American novelists, the best of whom was Faulkner, with his near-surrealist picture of our decaying South. The activist American temperament, so different from the European, made our novelists more prone to the theme of violence than that of sensitivity. There have been no Kafkas, no Prousts among us. But Hemingway's best works, gusto and bravura notwithstanding, bear witness to the modern absorption in death, failure, castration, lack of purpose — the centerless society. Fitzgerald attacked with more sensibility and genius the dangerous mores of materialism. His stories "The Diamond Big as the Ritz" and "The Rich Boy" show how clearly he understood the hollowness of acquisitiveness. *The Beautiful and the Damned,* and *The Great Gatsby* dramatize the destructive power of money. His intuition of some fatal flaw in the society was perhaps the most personal and deeply felt of all the writers of the period. His heroes shrink before our eyes, though they are still heroes, not non-heroes, still life size.

The many writers who went to Europe in disdain of

101

America were not writing of hope or health. At the same time, they were not yet, except for Faulkner, writing primarily of decay, and not in the mood of despair but of still hopeful antagonism. They separated themselves from society but did not completely denigrate it. The sense of disintegration was implicit, but not strong enough to shake the hubris of the American power elite to whom at any rate the art chart of the artists' approval or disapproval is of no moment. Even a great poetic work, with its all too accurate title, *"The Wasteland,"* could be shrugged off as more relevant to Europe than to ourselves.

But in 1929 a gigantic tremor shook the social system, and this could not be ignored nor fled from by the artists, since it was not brief and shook not only the United States but the whole western world. The Great Depression brought on another surge of fascism, this time in Germany where the economy and the morale had been weakened by war, aftermath of war, reparations and inflation. In America, the younger writers began to use their talents in the service of political propaganda. Sensitivity virtually vanished as a theme. The world had become too treacherous and too much in need of reform for sensitivity to have any value. The art of protest, which is inevitably a second-rate art, took over. The greater artist describes, has no real calling to reform, the world. When in 1933 we were faced with seventeen million unemployed, the best minds and spirits turned inevitably to action. And as the horrors progressed, through the Second World War, the mass murder of the Jews, the dropping of the atom bomb, the creation of art was left to smaller people, writing on smaller and more negative subjects, with new attitudes to which no great spirit could lend his allegiance.

Painters suffered from the same trauma. They found their one possible creative outlet, one that is denied to writers (in spite of some recent attempts by French novelists) — the channel of abstraction. They moved en masse toward the formal, non-human, safe levels. The meaning of the present was too disagreeable to express. As Paul Klee said, "The more horrible the world, the more abstract our art." The human face, in all its vulnerable sensitivity, had to be broken up into geometric symbols. Violence, brutality and despair emerged as meanings in plastic art for a time, but eventually almost all those who were painting had fled into the abstract, grotesque, remote or meaningless. Today, pop art is busy divesting art of meaning at any level. It is saying: there is no meaningful art in our society.

Many societies have stifled their artists. Soviet Russia has a wretched record in this regard. Its poets, cut off from free response to the scene, have committed suicide or have been destroyed in other ways by the foolishness of the activists in control of the country. There is some excuse for their rulers in their deep and well-founded fear of attack from the counter societies of the world among which the United States has been a leader. Yet they would now be in more safety if they had a fifty-year literary record of their artists' reactions to the hopes and difficulties and values of the revolution and its aftermath. For the Russians, as for the United States, a recognition of the accuracy of art in assessing the social scene could have prevented or at least modified the worst blunders of both sets of politicians, who are yet able out of this blindness to destroy all life on the globe.

It is true that the small themes of our day — small for a variety of reasons — develop no great creative figures in this country. But at least there are many small ones. Russia does not have even the benefit of free-wheeling art that could make clear what values its political performance has spread through the populace and how the deepest and most permanent layers of human biology, as found in the artist, react to the new way of life. In effect, the order to produce only social realism has all but obliterated the natural art flow in Russia.

It should perhaps be reiterated that one does not look to the artist to save the world through his opinions or his personal deeds. Only in rare periods can the artist operate as an activist and run in line with the general ideas of the time. Usually the artists watch from a large or small distance the activities of the rest of us. They are often neither practical nor logical. But their best works achieve as close to infallibility concerning the human condition as one could hope for. Even in the works of minor artists we can discover what is going on. Their constructions, their images in word, shape, color, sound can be ignored only at our peril; their retreats and silences indicate the greatest peril of all.

Though in this country literature has fared a little better than in Russia during the last twenty years, and there are varieties of voices, the general tone and quality of the modern novel as well as of the drama draws an ominous line on the chart. The words "alienation" and "absurd" have become the truisms of literary criticism; violence, mess, schizophrenia and despair have taken over the arena. If one reads the "absurd" novels, one is impressed with the cleverness of these writers who are taking this semi-abstract way of showing how it feels for creative people to live in this period. Perfection of spirit, expansion of sensibility are now lost causes, and "the point is that life doesn't have any point," to quote from the title of a recent article in the *Times Book Review*. The mood is strictly ironic; every aspect of life is reduced to the ridiculous, which might be construed as a technique to reduce the pain, fear or anger called forth to such a degree. The writers of this school are cool, ingenious and amusing. Pynchon's *V*, Heller's *Catch 22*, and Barth's *The Sot-weed Factor,* for example, are all tales in which a "human society is so cruel that individual man, no matter how strong his will, can find no salvation within it." Within this genre of alienation we find twisted portraits, caricatures describing man not as he is but as ridiculous. This sort of novel is a very mental, contrived performance, and the author is not pretending to create real people.

Another cult deriving from the pervasive sense of estrangement is more emotional, sometimes hysterical. Burroughs *Naked Lunch* is a deep retreat from the normal world. Such writers are using the terror-soaked material from their subconscious minds rather than playing amusing games with their characters, and their forms are apt to be surrealistic. This branch of alienation has strange blooms that give off an odor of decay.

These two trends have of course been even more obvious in the theater. The downward curve of our drama merits a quick look, especially since a play strikes more forcibly and directly at its audience and its very survival depends on whether it is what the audience wants to see and hear. Our stage for some time has been filled with feeble and pathetic creatures. We have come a long way from O'Neill's heroes, who were suffering to be sure, and disaffected by middle class values, but still heroes, down to the half-paralyzed no-men of today. In *Death of a Salesman*, the main character has already been destroyed by society when the curtain rises; in *The Connection* the stage is littered with human beings waiting for a drug fix. Beckett, whose *Waiting for Godot* depicted our era of absurd, grotesque, nightmarish stage images with a certain vigor and tragic form, is of course not an American, but an Irishman in the Joyce tradition, writing in French and English. His recent plays dehumanize man even further, and moreover often deny any body to the drama itself. Beckett seems to be deliberately reducing the richness of his own art.

It is logical that the alienation theme permeating our air should find its most adept writers among the alienated, or persecuted groups of our society: Irish, Jewish, Negro, deep poor, or the more personally dislocated homosexuals. Among these there are very talented but not large-voiced singers. In their stories the hero, like his stage counterpart, usually enters the scene with some fatal handicap over and above his sensibility. For now sensibility has become a burden, and the imagination an instrument of torture. The strong emotional tone of these writers and their serious understanding of estrangement gives their work greater status than the novels of the grotesque and the absurd. They belong in what Jonathan Baumback calls "the landscape of nightmare," in his recent book [1] on nine contemporary novelists. The novel of the '50's, he says, is generally involved with "personal culpability in a self-destroying civilization." The individual psyche is revealed at its darkest and most miserable. Herzog is half deranged when the book opens; others of Bellow's heroes are puny and helpless — the "victim," the "dangling man." Even his Henderson, for all his resemblance to a man of vitality, has half of his personality submerged in an icy wasteland dreamworld. Hawkes takes for his locale a decaying "no-land." Styron uses a Virginia full of madness and nightmare. Salinger's heroes are on their way to insanity; Ellison's "invisible man" lives in a madhouse world. The fine sensitivity of Wallant gives us the pathetic and hostile society of Moonbloom's tenants. Sickness is everywhere.

Because they are themselves entrenched in alienation, these writers have the interest and energy to deal with this essentially small, ego-corroding theme. The artists who were interested in glorifying sensitivity — Joyce, Mann, Proust, James — were of a prouder, entirely different order from those who today are intrigued by the decay and shrivelling of the psyche and the meaninglessness of existence, unredeemed by the animating vitality the older writers found in sensitivity.

[1] Jonathan Baumbach, *The Landscape of Nightmare* (New York University Press, 1965).

Today the greater artists, who might be writing on larger themes, are silent. This is not the kind of world they want to write about. The continuing decay of both capitalism and Christianity has been made even more disagreeable by the fear of the nuclear bomb. The whole human race seems to be at stake. The great artist operates from an attraction to life; no matter how critical he has been of his time, he has always found a way to describe it with a sort of passionate enjoyment, and with respect for the force within humanity. Today the sourness and fear in the air paralyze the finest sensibilities, and we are left with the sickly products of self-pity and estrangement.

There is one striking deviation on the chart of the twentieth century novel. One writer, Malraux, was describing courage and health of spirit, and purposefulness at a time when his contemporaries were unable to depict anything but sickness, wasteland and despair. It was undoubtedly Malraux's trip to the East and his participation in the Chinese revolution that made it possible for *Man's Fate* to be written. There he came in touch with a vitality and unity long missing from Europe. In the words of Haakon Chevalier, who wrote the introduction to his Modern Library translation of *Man's Fate* in 1934:

> "What is evoked throughout the novel is the central struggle of modern times — the struggle of a dying order with the forces that are molding a new world. . . . The war gave us a literature of heroism. But it was a heroism of despair. These men died bravely but they died in vain. Upon that whole catastrophe

108

there hangs the blight of a ghastly futility. The heroes of *Man's Fate* are valid for our time because they live, work and meet their death in pursuit of a goal to which the future of humanity is intimately linked."

Malraux's novel transcended the proletarian literature of the thirties. He gave us the first full-scale, direct attack on the capitalist world, using the businessman's own invention — the art form of the novel. To this our social system has made no reply; no artist has risen to affirm our ruling values or to find any purpose in "the struggle of a dying order." Since *Man's Fate* was written, the stature of man, as he has come through the images of our artists, has become shrunken and stooped. He is as thin in literature as in matchstick figures of Giacometti. The imagination seems to be unable to produce any fullbodied images of human life in our culture.

It has always been assumed that art is useful in making us aware of what life was truly like in the past. This has proved to be a rather useful and dependable idea. By the same token the art chart can be put to work on more current soundings. The complaining quality in the verbal arts in the United States has been unremitting for over forty years. From "The Wasteland" on, this chorus has been swelling, to reach full blast in the nightmare scream of today's fiction. If we can take our eyes off the business chart for a brief moment to take a look at the more permanent art chart, we find a dangerous split. The "great society" goes one way and its artists another. The artist may be feeble in the world of affairs but in his works he gives a true picture of the psychic mood of his day. Much painful blundering could be avoided if power could be made to listen to sensibility.

Sartre and Camus show that life in a centerless society is absurd. Not man but the social scene is responsible for existentialism. A new set of values, a new unity both religious and political is imminent. It has been predicted by philosophers and scientists from all sides of skepticism. As Frank Manuel writes in his *Shapes of Philosophical History:*

"Even the circular philosophers of history or cultural sociologists who hold fast to an iron law of the circle from which there is no release, men like Spengler and Sorokin, nevertheless testify that the next period will see a rebirth of spirit. The contemporary civilization of gigantism, sensation, and technics has exhausted its creative capabilities and a new ideational, mystical or religious form is about to be born somewhere. . . .

As a member of the generation of 1910 I have seen my fill of horror in war and peace. . . . In the midst of universal dread of nuclear annihilation, world-wide social revolution, internecine racial wars, the spectacle of fat-land inhabitants committing suicide by over-feeding and of barren lands incapable of preventing the mass starvation of the hungry, the assurances of the prophets of the new spirituality often seem utopian, even a hollow joke. The victims of the twentieth century slaughterhouse refuse to believe it.

As a skeptic I am reluctant to receive the witness of the heralds of the new spirit, and yet it is pouring in

110

upon me from so many diverse sources and directions
that I am on the point of surrendering my belief in the
ordinary evidence of the senses."[1]

Our "centerless," "disaffected," "alienated," "uncommitted" and disappointed society has naturally developed
many neurotic artists, and this has built up the conception
of these gifted beings as peculiar, eccentric and anti-social.
This is an especially American myth, and one that automatically perpetuates itself. A united society, with an
accepted iconography, and devoted people working for it,
gets healthy artists as we saw in the Italian Renaissance
and in the era of great Dutch painting. The next century
will undoubtedly see an effort, based neither on capitalism
nor on old time religion, to find a unifying central purpose
for our diverse and distracted world. In this new movement,
art will play a major role.

[1] (Stanford University Press, 1965), pp. 160-2.

V

SCIENCE
AND
ART

Science and art emerge from different areas of the human mind. While a form of imagination is at work in both, there is a vast difference between them in scope and emotional tone. For science virtually eliminates the sensuous level; it inhabits the abstracting, intellectual part of the brain and operates by means of mathematical forms. It clarifies and puts to use for man the material universe. It is true that the excitement of scientific discovery sometimes gives a pleasure comparable to the aesthetic joy. But this lasts only as long as the process of verification is going on, and is a joy granted only to the very few. There is no concrete object left, with the individual's stamp on it, that can stimulate and please great numbers of people — however useful a scientific discovery may be in expediting daily life. A paraphrase of the original work, a formula, a new mathematical relationship wrested from nature to be absorbed and passed on into the next experimentation — such is the non-personal, non-sensuous legacy of science.

Science does not create new relationships. It finds and measures the old ones in the light of new methods. A work of art, on the other hand, is a new, distinctly personal and human construction suspended between the abstract intellectual concept and the chaotic heap of nature. In this ambivalent area, there are limitless possibilities of complexity and originality, as the artist grasps at elements of sound and sight in order to create expressive objects for the pleasure of other human beings. A work of art is symmetrically inexact, in some degree taxing. It is held together, like the human mind itself, by a special unique pattern that has its own orientation to reality. Because of its inclusiveness, because it emerges from all levels of the artist's biology and is animated by the sensuous as well as the intellectual drive, it appeals to us on all levels. It is so thoroughly tuned to our biology that it can change radically our perception of ourselves and of the outside world.

A painter's invention can transform our vision of space; a musician can illuminate, through his rhythms, assonance, dissonance, the psychic strains of our existence, or the equilibrium which he has found through his own special insight. What he creates can affect deeply our attitudes, purposes and emotional fortitude. A scientific genius can change the direction of physics, biology and astronomy, he can undermine religions by his theories, and stimulate research that has enormous consequence in the world of action. But he has no impact on the sensibilities of the majority of men, who cannot respond to the mathematical formulas that make his theories possible. Nor would they necessarily increase their value as human beings if they could understand them. A scientist changes the environment; the artist affects human nature. The artist speaks to

116

all men because his communication is animate, sensuous, still heated with the feelings and emotions that are barred from scientific creation once it is completed and put to practical use in the world of action.

The emotion of curiosity which excites the scientist on his road to discovery is not transferred to his material. It remains wholly within himself. The impact of a scientific experiment, as it is for instance presented to the student, is gone after a single viewing; one does not return again and again, as one does to art, for the pleasure of repeating the experience. The material is cold, reaching us not through our senses but indirectly through conceptual thinking. Facts are arranged, and uniformities are found, but no fixed sensuous images remain. The object of science is not to make nature memorable through imagery nor to reveal aspects of our psychological reality through emotional experience. Its purpose is to straighten out and organize our knowledge of reality and present its form and process pure and bare of feeling. This is why, as scientific research tackles problems involving human consciousness, its power to discover and verify laws weakens. It is at its best when dealing with the abstractions that relate to the oldest forms and rhythms of the universe — the rules governing the non-animal, non-conscious base of our world. Here measurement has its greatest triumphs. The unique, one-of-a-kind human being and the one-of-a-kind work of art do not submit to formula or sliderule. The laboratory is of little use in defining more than general physiological and psychological attributes.

The psychologist gropes for knowledge of the psyche

with the tools of scientific logic, but it is the artist who succeeds in giving a home to the complex relationships that make man unique. The artist feels, with all his biological equipment, toward discovery of the present and future human fate. The scientist is busy rationalizing the past, and creating more and more intellectual tools for manipulation of the material world and of society. The artist pursues realization, the scientist knowledge. The latter has performed the great function of destroying old misconceptions of nature, and has brought us somewhat nearer to the truth about our origins and our complicated structure. It is the scientific imagination which has set to work on the mysteries of chromosome, gene, enzymes, DNA, RNA and proteins, atoms, ions, organelles, and all that may mean for the control and improvement of the race. But scientists are in no way equipped to substitute new values for the old superstitions they have destroyed and which, in the shape of religions, provided food for men's emotions and motives for their behavior. Even the social scientists who deal with the complete human being cannot communicate in such a way as to set up any real goals. The kinetic warmth that affects and transforms the human psyche is missing from the scientific imagination.

While the artist's judgment and methods must always be tentative, less orderly than the scientist's, he is more likely to get closer to psychic reality than the man of statistics and formulas. There have been the great insights into the nature of man from Socrates to Freud and the new biologically-oriented philosophers such as de Chardin, but the esoteric nature of the material has always militated against any true understanding by the majority — the medium is too special to convey the message. The abstraction of the "unconscious" for example, in spite of all the lip service it is given, remains as mysterious as Time-Space to all but the initiated few who have found it a workable theory. For the rest of mankind, the destructive element of psycho-analysis has outbalanced its very real values. Science destroys illusions, but is not prepared nor intended to provide the psychic energy that will carry us on without them. It can clear away debris from our minds but cannot evoke the total psychic response. The light generated by a novel like *The Brothers Karamazov,* the intimate realization of human nature in all its distortion, frailty and greatness could never be equalled by the application of any general laws, or psychoanalytical techniques.

Art, because of the admixture of the sensuous, becomes at its greatest organic, and in a special way alive. The three levels from which it springs parallel the three levels of the mind that receives it. Its messages move quickly, one might say electrically, from man to man. A new feeling, a new hope, a new purpose — these are transmitted through art at certain times, as are also sickness and despair. Art is immediate, and not subject to correction or verification. Scientists live in a slower, colder world, where there are indeed wonders, but they are found rather than created. Their discoveries are provisional and sequential, not final. Nothing unique has been added; a facet of the universe has been opened up and explained. Two scientists can make precisely the same discovery. Two artists, however, because they are using their whole personalities in the act

119

of creation, and because they differ biologically, cannot make the same work of art.

Art is more than a logical trial and error process, more than a mental effort to find order, and to understand what makes everything tick. It proceeds from man's greatest gift which is to originate, to variegate his own nature, to add a new element beyond the known relationships. A rabbit finding his way out of a maze is an experimental scientist on a low level. But the rabbit is an artist on no level at all. It takes more than the exploratory drive and the careful working out of all possibilities to make the artist. Because he is using the total unique complexity of his being, including tiers of intuition evolved through centuries of biological evolution, the images the artist gives us are inevitably as complex as himself and point to the complexities of future generations.

Among the functions of the human imagination, humor and science bear an interesting similarity. They both proceed from the conceptual, colder, comparison-making, puzzle-solving area of our minds. The humorist presents us with a situation that seems headed in a sure direction and then suddenly diverts us by another idea cutting across his equation contrary to expectation. The suddenness with which the incongruity jolts us releases tension that spills over into laughter. Our concept of the situation has been upset, usually to the chagrin and denigration of some other person. Any emotional involvement is cut off. Freed from the need to work out the problem, and safe in our detachment from it, we feel relieved and pleased. It's only a joke, after all.

This sudden sharp suspension of the comparison-making our minds are forever engaged in provides somewhat the same relief and pleasurable variety as a discovery. A mental set is upset; there is a gap between what we expect and what we encounter. Where the gap is slight, some will find nothing funny in it. And where it is very great, some will not make the connection at all. That is one reason why the sense of humor differs so widely among individuals. The other reason is that a joke is constructed entirely on the mathematical formal level, and is devoid of any feeling content, so that for persons who are unable to shut themselves off from the area of their sensibility, sympathy will inhibit laughter at an incongruity which involves cruelty and discomfort to the person at the wrong end of the joke. Humor is one of the most efficient ways to shut off emotion, but there are immense variations in our ability or desire to make this escape.

In scientific research we also find escape from emotional tension. But there is a difference in that with a joke there is only one comparison to be made: between the normal expectation and the surprise twist at the end. Whereas in scientific work there are many possible roads the investigation might take and they appear right at the start of the experience instead of at the end. A scientific problem starts out with a job of reconciliation to be done, and ends with a gap bridged. Many ideas have to be explored to build this bridge which will fit the problem into a new conceptual scheme. There may be intensity in the hunt for the solution, but other emotions are not involved. The serious business of fitting the concepts together does not terminate suddenly in an unexpected incongruity, but the search and expectation continue steadily until there is a union of the old and the new that is logically satisfying. We are relieved and pleased at the working out of the solution. Tension is released. Where humor makes us laugh at incongruity, science provides the contentment of congruity. Both are conceptual, abstract rearrangements, involving only a section of the human personality.

Neither a joke book nor a scientific treatise (nor even a flight toward Mars) works on our full biological nature. The conceptualizing, the abstract formulas involved leave us mostly uninvolved. Pure intellectual discovery, making unities of theoretical divergences, is not an operation that engages all of our human capacities. Neither the jokemaker who separates concepts nor the scientist who joins them are fully creative; their inventions are two-dimensional, somewhat thin, spun from the wits and not the whole man. The curiosity drive can be satisfied on a level that involves only part of us — the part that we use in daily life when we are constantly at work to make patterns fit. For scientists this activity is more persistent and continuous, going on even in sleep.

Humor too is essential in our daily life. It represents, as Koestler says: "a level of evolution . . . . where reasoning had gained a certain degree of autonomy from the 'blind' urges of emotion; where thought had acquired that independence and nimbleness which enable it to detach itself from feeling." [1] Humor is a cooling process and a valuable control.

[1] Koestler, *op. cit.*, p. 63.

The control of science over our environment is of course extremely powerful and pervasive. It is doubtful whether human evolution could have occurred without man's intellectual curiosity and the drive to organize and manipulate nature. Whether this happened along the lines of Darwinian external adaptation or through the "internal selection" that Lancelot Law Whyte suggests in his stimulating recent book [1] is something we must leave to the geneticists and philosophers of science. But it looks as if the next evolutionary step will also depend in part on intellectual curiosity and perhaps in part on man's drive to manipulate himself now that he has learned so much control over nature. Without science, man would not have the tools to make improvements in the general sensibility of mankind which seems to be now so much more vital to human survival than the power drive. Modern biological research into the brain structure, as well as into the cells that control heredity with their complicated chemistry, may herald an epoch in which we will be able to influence the quality as well as the size of the world population. This concept has its terror as well as it hope. The biologist Dr. Philip Siekevitz was quoted in an article in the *New York Times* in July, 1963 as saying: [2]

> "We are now approaching the greatest event in human history, even in the history of life on earth, the deliberate changing by man of many of his biological

[1] *Internal Factors in Evolution* (George Braziller, 1965), p. 23: "The internal structure of organisms has directly influenced the avenues of phylogeny."

[2] William L. Laurence, "Gains in Biology."

123

processes. . . . We will be able to plan ahead so that our children will be what we like them to be — physically and even mentally. At that point man will be remodeling his own being."

This next step must be planned by man, he said, "with some purpose in mind — a concept of the future to give meaning to his fateful moves."

There are many enlightened and conscientious scientists, but science itself, as it moves forward, is and must be spiritually indifferent. While it can discover infinite possibilities and directions, it is not equipped to judge their value for human beings or for human society. It is essential to science that it be free to make its trials and its errors. It is up to men in other fields to make the effort to discover which roads that science uncovers are the most usable, which are too dangerous, and which will further the increase in sensibility that will keep us from destroying ourselves. Science left to its own devices without a humanistic control, would create a macabre society with no purpose except more and more power over the environment, until ultimately neglect of the human factors would destroy that environment.

Of all those called on to balance the surge of science, the artist seems the most trustworthy. His indirect, quiet but unremitting awareness of human needs, conditions, emotions, and above all his power to communicate with others in all their varying psychic states, make the true complement, the missing half of the scientific man. We go to the physicists and chemists for further exploration of the universe, to the physician for our bodies, to the engineers for shelter, machines, bridges, space travel. We need the lawyers, journalists, social scientists and mathematicians to keep our complicated society going. But if we want to know what is happening to the human spirit, we must go to the artist. He is the soundest interpreter, if only because this is his essential task. Like the philosopher, he conceives of the world in terms of meanings rather than means, but unlike the philosopher he creates communicative objects, products of his sense organs and his wits, that make him a messenger to and from the less articulate. He is gifted with extraordinary psychic ability; if he is not rejected, he can help the scientist lead us to the next plateau of human evolution.

Science, moving deliberately within the discipline of its two levels — cognition and mathematical form — is capable of closer and closer analysis of our biological make-up and the energy that makes it live. But art, functioning freely on all levels of the human consciousness, expresses the latent and imminent aspects of our fate. It is the cutting edge of our biological awareness. Its interpretations should be taken seriously, especially at a time when, as a biologist tells us, we will soon have to answer a new question. No longer, what creature is man?, but what creature should he become?

VI

CHANGING
MAN

C H A P T E R   S I X

"Every authentic function of the human spirit has this decisive characteristic . . . it does not merely copy but rather embodies an original formative power. It does not express passively the mere fact that something is present, but contains an independent energy of the human spirit. . . . This is as true of art as it is of cognition; it is as true of myth as of religion."

Ernst Cassirer
The Philosophy of Symbolic Forms

On most charts, whether of life expectancy, art, or economics, we expect rises and falls. But there is one phenomenon that is assumed to be enduring and consistent — religion. And it is not easy for many people to make the assumption that in this as in all matters human, there is a rise and fall. But just as man lives and dies, so all his establishments have a life cycle and religions, too, have their mortality.

Old centers of faith do not break up without struggle, pain and violence. But break they must, to make way for new faith and new purposes. That has been our pattern in the western world ever since Homer voiced the first faint doubt about the holy omnipotence of the Greek gods — doubt that was to culminate about five hundred years later in the killing of Socrates. That was the fifth century B.C., and two thousand years later, as another cluster of beliefs was loosening, Giordano Bruno was burned at the stake for his reservations about the Christian dogma and his belief that there were other worlds besides ours. Between these two martyrs to the questioning of old faiths, Christ was killed for his affirmation of a new faith. Western man punishes with violence those at the extremes of either belief or unbelief, and fears the new as much as loss of the old. This fear is still strong, and its effects still merciless.

For in spite of all resistance to change, faiths have definite life spans. Only the concept of a god seems to be built permanently into our psyches, and lasts through all cultures. As Kenneth Burke wrote, there is a god term in the integument of every language.[1] Theology on the other hand rises and falls, and it seems to have gone through its swiftest permutations in the Mediterranean world. European history shows that there has always been a strong tendency to search the sky for some new enlightenment, this search following on a pronounced boredom with an extreme of belief or of unbelief. For a chaotic disunity and looseness of purpose can bore men as much as the prison of dogma. Also, intellectual curiosity may develop

[1] Kenneth Burke, *The Rhetoric of Religion* (Beacon Press, 1961), p. 2.

faster among peoples close to the sea with easy access through travel and commerce to other lands and new ideas. This communication throughout the Mediterranean area may have prevented the solidification and steadier state of religious faiths such as occurs on a large continental mass like India or China. Dogma breaks up sooner where cross currents make men aware of differing concepts and new discoveries.

In the two cycles that we can trace clearly, the Greek and the Christian, there is a striking similarity in duration and in the pattern of disintegration. Just before Homer, (roughly 1,000 B.C.) the gods were flourishing. One can detect in the two Homeric epics of 900 B.C. a microscopic hint of skepticism. Aeschylus (525-456 B.C.) still took the gods for granted. One generation later, Sophocles showed the first open doubt, and Euripides, farther into the fifth century, had definitely lost reverence. By 399 B.C., the establishment had become sufficiently alarmed to put to death the prime unabashed heretic, Socrates. He was a culmination of doubt, and like Bruno later, a martyr to intellectual integrity. Both Socrates and Bruno were victims of existing in a time when doubts about the old religion were growing but not yet accepted. After Socrates, the Greek religion became so debilitated that Aristophanes was able to make a laughing stock of the gods right on the stage without fear of reprisals. Strong central faith was gone, and gone also the great period of Greek art which came just before the old gods died.

After a few hundred years of disunity, decadence and chaos, at the pole of zero faith, men found existence

131

insupportable, and a new religion was born with the crucifixion of Christ. There were more martyrs, but by the fifth century A.D. it was a conquering faith and there were no more penalties for following it. St. Augustine's life illustrates how safe it is to be engaged in solidifying a religion that is well on its way to acceptance, though another five hundred years had to pass before Christianity was widespread and unchallenged throughout Europe. The millenium of growth and consolidation was complete by the 11th century — corresponding to 1,000 B.C. in the Greek cycle, the moment of full tide of belief.

Then, inevitably, the tide began slowly to recede. By the 15th century there began to be doubts about the value of the next world versus this one, a concept that had been so important in the dark ages after the break-up of the Roman Empire. A new comet appeared in the sky — science — the inevitable evolutionary surge of man's intellectual curiosity questioning the myths he himself had made. By the end of the 15th century, Bruno was burned at the stake because the Christian Church, feeling the threat of science, began to fight for its survival like a living thing.

It was during the two centuries preceding that the European renaissance in art occurred. Again there is a pronounced resemblance to the Greek cycle. The highest period in Greek art began about 500 B.C., when Aeschylus was twenty-five years old. Phidias lived from 490 to 416 B.C. and was only twenty-one years older than Socrates. The two great renaissances preceded the two religious killings and in both cycles, moreover, art ceased to support religion during the years when the unifying supernatural beliefs disintegrated and it was far too soon for another faith to fill the vacuum.

Art seems to reach its high points during periods of faith but just when that faith is beginning to slacken and new ideas are generating excitement, and when men out of boredom and stultification let loose their passion for innovation and variety. Art is tied up with this evolutionary urge toward novelty. Artists, who paradoxically must feel in some degree secure in order to create, are the most extreme innovators, and closer to the pulse of change than other men, sooner aware of the approach of a new comet that must be fitted into the established system. The ferment caused by the impact of the unknown, fresh idea on the traditional stimulates the production of art. The painters and sculptors of the 15th and 16th centuries were still operating from the safe platform of Christian belief, but their works were already beginning to burgeon with new feelings and new conceptions having to do with the natural world instead of the supernatural. By the 16th century men had almost shaken off their long dark preoccupation with the hierarchies of heaven and hell and were concentrating more on this life than on the hereafter. Artists, sometimes half-scientists like Leonardo, discovered new laws and techniques. Under the thin disguise of religious subjects, they experimented with perspective and color and painted flesh and blood and the forms of nature with a realism that had been absent from art for a thousand years.

Little by little, devotion to a faith held in common gave way to individualism. In the end a painting no longer went by the religious subject, but by the name of the artist, and

133

it was created not for the glory of God, but for another sort of glory much nearer at hand. Patrons began to buy a name, not a Last Supper or a Virgin. The tide of religious intensity and mysticism was on its way out, and disintegration of belief had begun. During the four hundred years since the Renaissance we have again been approaching the pole of zero faith that was the climate of the year one A.D. By the next century, the Christian theology will probably be (as it is already for artists, intellectuals and some churchmen*) in the same category as the Greek gods during the days of the late Roman Empire. The ethic at the core of Christ's teaching will survive, even as the mythology dies. For the ideal of compassion and brotherly love is as surely a process in the evolution of consciousness and as permanent a part of the collective psyche as the concept of one god contributed by the Jewish religion.

The Christian establishment, however, can no longer control the doubts raised by science. It has little leverage for its myths in a world of universal education, prodigious communication and economic plenty. It was born into a time when nature, including human nature, was a menace, and when a good half of mankind was slave to the other half. It was in part a religion of scarcity, a response to physical and spiritual need. It grouped men together again around a shared miracle, gave them another world to look forward to, a holy family to worship, and more miracles to make life in this world even supportable. Self-respect

---

* As clearly indicated in "The New Theologian" by Ved Mehta, *The New Yorker,* November, 1965.

and hope for the after life were the gifts of Christ to the needy and brutish populations left bobbing in the wake of the Roman Empire. Men were drawn to the supernatural, as they have always been, for the succor and relief provided by an illusion.

Now, almost two thousand years later, nature has been tamed if not mastered. Human consciousness has spread in scope; masses of men have some sort of scientific knowledge and are thereby less vulnerable to exploitation. There is some hope for material security. Social reform that developed originally from the Christian ethic seems to have become a permanent value; equality is preached even when not practiced. Promise of happiness in the next life to make up for deprivation in this one does not have the same lure in a society where promises of immediate relief are made continually and often kept.

As for the next life itself — just as Socrates undermined the old Olympus, so physics and mathematics and chemistry and the social sciences have shattered the myths of heaven and hell, devils and angels, the Last Judgment, the creation of man and woman on a certain day. In spite of fear and resistance, evolution is now taken for granted by the majority. As J. C. Smuts wrote as far back as 1926:

> "Today I think it is generally accepted that life has in the process of cosmic evolution developed from or in the bosom of material. I do not think that among those who have given thought and attention to these matters there are today any who seriously question this position. Life is no dove that has flown to our shores from some world beyond this world; mind or soul is not an

importation from some other universe. Life and mind are not mere visitants *to* this world but not *of* this world. There is nothing alien in them to the substance of the universe; they are with us and they are of us." [1]

Since that was written, science has begun to make a synthesis of the three levels of matter, life, self-consciousness, and perhaps in the not too distant future will be able to define the gap between life and non-life. Such research is completely foreign to our religious institutions; and their arsenals for defense are still full of the superstitions and taboos which they have used for centuries to keep law and order. But the course of science cannot be checked. Already the need to control births is bringing on a minor crisis in the Catholic system. Even farther out into forbidden territory, biologists are exploring the possibility of changing the quality of the population as well as its size. The idea that man will some day be able to breed out the recurrent weaknesses, handicaps and ghastly mistakes that plague every generation through inheritance of faulty genes is still repugnant to most people regardless of religion, education or common sense. But it is an idea entirely consistent with biological evolution. Ancient fears stand in the way, but it is conceivable that some future faith, centered around the development of higher sensibilities will make use of this scientific tool.

Herman J. Muller, one of the contributors to *The*

[1] Smuts, *op. cit.*, pp. 7-8.

Control of Human Heredity and Evolution,[1] discusses the possibility of "germinal choice," in other words parental selection of germ plasm from "established banks of stored germ cells (spermatozoa) . . . derived from persons of very diverse types but including as far as possible those whose lives had given evidence of outstanding gifts of mind, merits of disposition and character." He is perhaps too hopeful about the acceptance of the idea:

"It has been estimated that thousands of children per year are engendered in the United States by artificial insemination of women whose husbands are sterile with sperm derived from donors. The choosing of these donors is always carried out solely by the clinician, and their identity is kept strictly secret from the couple concerned. . . .

Undoubtedly many of the couples who have resorted to this procedure would have jumped at the chance of having their child derived from germinal material of unusual promise, and some of them would have even have had the courage not to dissimulate about their enterprise. This would in turn give encouragement to those realistic idealists who, though not burdened by sterility or unusual defect, would actually prefer to have a child who had resulted from the exercise of their studied choice, rather than risk the still greater uncertainties of favorable outcome that natural procreation would have entailed. My experience with

[1] Edited by T. M. Sonnenborn. *The Control of Human Heredity and Evolution,* "Means and Aims" by H. J. Muller (Macmillan, New York, 1965), pp. 115-6.

137

talking with people on this subject has convinced me Americans are not such a nation of sheep in this respect and that, if the opportunity of germinal choice were opened, a gradually increasing number of seemingly 'normal' couples, in addition to a large proportion of those afflicted with seminal inadequacy or obvious genetic defect, would elect to use this means of having at least a part of their family. Moreover, as the saying goes, 'nothing succeeds like success' and the obvious successes achieved by this method would within a generation win it still more adherents. It would constitute a major extension of human freedom in a quite new direction."

The "gifts of mind, merits of disposition and character" which Mr. Muller wants for the sperm bank are pretty vague terms and open to many interpretations. Certainly gifts of sensibility and artistic power should be included as equally important. The scientist is naturally slanted toward the development of the scientific imagination and the mind which, like his own, is dominated by logic. The artist, with his image-forming abilities and his more readily available subconscious stores, should play a large role in any program to add a dimension to human nature through what is now called "tampering" with the genes. Moreover, in estimating values for the society, the artist would not be apt to be as arbitrary or as experimental as the scientist. Where the logical mind may blunder, the intuitive mind with its accessibility to our past biological history is likely to lead to safer experiments. The emphasis of the scientist on the higher mental centers alone makes for a detachment from the total sense-grounded self, and he is able to put forth a highly plausible but erroneous theory that might lead us into the dead end of human prodigy and monstrosity. The artist while less logical has more balance. His work must be true to the total man, to all elements that make up our consciousness — he is not, like the scientist, freewheeling. His intuition of wholeness, the quality that can produce a poem or painting able to stir us on all levels, is an essential counterbalance to the brilliant, not quite human logic of the experimenting scientist.

Resistance to experimenting with human heredity will persist, to be overcome perhaps only by a new religious tide surging in to fill the present spiritual vacuum. Some mystic some day may pronounce it our holy duty to promote our own evolution and thus fulfill God's purposes, calling for a crusade in laboratory and studio to edge man in that direction. The place of art will then be more deeply understood, itself one of the rites of the new faith. Art will be recognized as part of the secret of evolution in its function of stretching our consciousness, in its ability to add something unknown to our lives, something unique that does not respond to numbers or measurement, a new psychic dimension.

The relationship between art and religion has always existed. Malraux, writing of the psychology of art, traces this relation in all its subtleties from the most ancient to modern art. Frank Manuel, in his brilliant interpretive essay on Malraux, quotes from *The Voices of Silence*:

"Akin to all styles that express the transcendental and

139

unlike all others, our style seems to belong to some religion of which it is unaware. Yet it owes its affinity with the former not to the expression of faith in an unseen world, as it were, but, rather, to the absence of such faith, and as it were a photographic negative of the styles of the transcendent."

Malraux saw modern art, according to Mr. Frank, as an

"unprecedented effort to restore art's immemorial link with the sacred in a desacralized world."[1]

Art like religion comes from the level of the deep mysteries: life, death, basic urges to grow, basic fears. Art renaissances spring up at a certain point in the religious cycle; art seems to need the security and supporting medium of a center of faith around it, though rising to its best heights when the center of unity begins to loosen, threatened by exciting new ideas. Religions take a long time growing and dying. Other centers of belief, more mundane and shallow, such as nationalism, or capitalism or communism, fill less profound needs and their cycles are shorter. Yet even these truncated religions create minor renaissances of art, especially in their early stages of disintegration when creative ideas begin to invade and change their rigid forms.

We saw this phenomenon in the flowering of the novel at the end of the last century when faith in capitalism was just beginning to wane; (see Chap. IV). And the Irish renaissance of this century is an example of a short intense

[1] Joseph Frank, *The Widening Gyre* (Rutgers University Press, N. J., 1963), p. 93.

excitement created by a dying burst of nationalism. It produced its great artists: Yeats, Joyce, Synge, O'Casey. But this minor religious fervor died quickly, having hardly stirred the thick pall of the old Catholicism that encloses Ireland. An Ireland free is still an Ireland half asleep. Nationalism as a faith does not touch men's depths and has no staying power compared to religion.

Man is now again approaching the pole of zero faith, as we near the end of the two thousand year cycle of Christianity. T. S. Eliot, writing his great epic between two World Wars — and he himself both an American and an Englishman — dramatized the disunity, fear, decadence and despair of a civilization without a spiritual center. His title, "The Wasteland," was a portent and a warning long before the atom bomb turned fear into terror and gave us nightmares such as primitive man probably suffered in the face of hostile nature. Eliot was entirely accurate in his vision of our dying religions — the major one of Christianity and the newer, minor value system of capitalism — and it was hubris to ignore his revelation of the truth.

Eliot later, however, in his call for a return to unity, made the mistake of looking for an answer in the old and worn-out Christian myth, trying as it were to patch up a tower in the wasteland he knew so well instead of seeking a more promising land and a more feasible central faith. For we have our disunity and despair precisely because Christianity ceased many years ago to fit our knowledge of reality. Eliot's intuition of the chaos to come and his yearning for security forced him into retreat. By this he extended the wasteland instead of turning toward the future and a new synthesis, and bolstered Christianity's refusal to yield its place. Eliot was looking for a center in the wrong direction — in the past — ignoring the thousand years of change that must be absorbed into any new surge of spiritual energy, shutting his eyes to the fact that any religion, because it is man-made and man-supported, is mortal.

When the Christian synthesis began to crack, several hundred years ago, men began the exploration of the world around them, probing everything from the depths of earth and ocean to the movement and chemistry of the stars. This exploratory passion has reached its extreme now in our desperate interest in the interstices of the human mind. Both Proust and Freud, as two outstanding examples of psychological adventurers, have carried us to the painful extremity of individual diverseness and isolated self-consciousness. When men are unified around some pole of common belief, the individual is not scrutinized so minutely. We have gone very far with this exploration of the mystery of mind that has grown out of, and now self-consciously contemplates, its own nature. The weight of our diversities has become too onerous. Men grow tired, and long for the support of a group consciousness. There is much evidence that the search for unity is beginning again.

The old religion — so well established — dies slowly. The timid and the terrified cling to it. But it must die for the new to grow, and the new should now not be far off. Our artists in their despair and retreat confirm that we are at our lowest ebb of morale. Journalists and philosophers predict that a new tide is approaching. Paul Johnson wrote

142

in *The New Statesman* (September, 1965): "Maybe the time is ripe for an entirely new religion — the first since Mohammed." Arnold Toynbee tells us that our age has had about all the diversity it can take, and that we are now at a time when a new unity must be found. Even Sartre, arch-dramatist of the meaningless, wrote:

> "God is dead, but man has not, for all that, become atheistic. The silence of the transcendent, and the permanent need for religion in modern man — that is still the major thing. . . ."[1]

Whatever the new unity may be, it is certain that it must embrace the discoveries and advances in knowledge that helped destroy the old unity. A fresh faith, if it comes, must be based not so much on the supernatural but on the natural world which science has uncovered. We have come far from the old religions of the jungle, from the fetishes and animism, from many gods, even from one who is mythic. Religions, like the gods, have changed with the spread of human consciousness. Post-scientific age beliefs must have the odor of science. Our next unity will be built on something not as truncated as communism nor as mystic as shamanism, nor as mythic as Christ's divinity. It would be enough if we were to aim at invading and controlling man's psychic future on this earth in our reach toward man's divinity — there is sufficient mysticism in this alone. Any culture that produces a Catholic biologist-philosopher who speaks of "an unresolved simplicity,

[1] Jean Paul Sartre, *Situations* (George Braziller, 1965).

luminous in nature and not to be defined in terms of figures"[1] has gone well beyond the need for saints and myths. Who knows what insight some coming biologist, unveiling the secrets of evolution in his laboratory, might not have to offer as a meaning for living? The day of the appeal to the ancient superstitious animal in us is over. Our next religion will grow out of both science and art. No one can predict exactly how it will be born, but we do know that it cannot be a blind faith. We have become too conscious to approach the essentials of life and death with an entirely unintellectual approach; only science, empirically and mathematically, can provide us with the materials of a new faith: the phenomena of evolution proving that man is mutant, and capable of further heights. Yet religion is not born in a laboratory. It is an emotional transformation, a battle against old gods, and there will undoubtedly be martyrs dying for it. It is still too early to guess who they will be, though we can to a degree guess what they will be fighting for.

How does this sort of transformation come about? The last moment in European history when men were united around a passionate faith was in the eleventh and twelfth centuries, when all hearts, all crafts and especially all arts were involved in the worship of an unseen power. The

[1] ". . . the evolution of matter in our current theory comes back to the gradual building up by growing complication of the various elements recognized by physical chemistry. To begin with, at the very bottom there is still an unresolved simplicity, luminous in nature and not to be defined in terms of figures." Teilhard de Chardin, *The Phenomenon of Man* (Harper & Row, N. Y., 1961), p. 47.

144

building of the cathedrals was a stretching of abilities and energies in a common cause such as never occurred since. Henry Adams has described this welling-up of group creativity in his superb *Mont-Saint-Michel and Chartres:*

> "The whole Mount still kept the grand style: it expressed the unity of Church and State, God and Man, Peace and War, Life and Death, Good and Bad; it solved the whole problem of the universe. The priest and soldier were both at home here, in 1215 as in 1115 or in 1058; the politician was not outside of it; the sinner was welcome; the poet was made happy in his own spirit. . . . God reconciles all. The world is in evident harmony."[1]

Though art was produced, it was not produced by "artists" in our sense of the word. Individualism had not appeared. As Jean Gimpel tells us, in her book *The Cathedral Builders,*

> "The sculptors were lost among the general mass of stonecutters. This is really rather extraordinary to us, because an enormous difference seems to exist between those who perform a seemingly mechanical task, such as cutting blocks of stone, and those who sculpt, *with their very soul,* the magnificent statues in the cathedrals. The truth is that for the great majority of men in the Middle Ages there was between a good *work* and a *masterpiece* only a difference of degree, not a difference

[1] Henry Adams, *Mont-Saint-Michel and Chartres* (Houghton Mifflin, 1930), p. 44.

of kind. The idea that there is an unbridgeable gulf between a worker and an artist (in the modern sense of the word) did not really occur until the Renaissance when it was expressed by intellectuals who judged, classified and evaluated manual labor which was very foreign to them."[1]

Not only the blunt laborer, the artisan and artistic genius were drawn into the miracle of the 11th and 12th centuries. The moneyed upper class made astounding sacrifices. Henry Adams, in a passage aimed at his materialistic American readers, reveals what excesses of spending in the name of faith were indulged in by the hard-headed French:

"The measure of this devotion, which proves to any religious American mind, beyond possible cavil its serious and practical reality, is the money it cost. According to statistics, in the single century between 1170 and 1270, the French built eighty cathedrals and nearly five hundred churches of the cathedral class, which would have cost, according to an estimate made in 1840, more than five thousand millions to replace. Five million francs is a thousand million dollars, and this covered only the great churches of a single century. . . . The share of this capital which was — if one may use a commercial figure — invested in the Virgin cannot be fixed, any more than the total sum given to the religious objects between 1000 and 3000; but in a spiritual and artistic sense, it was almost the whole, and

[1] Jean Gimpel, *The Cathedral Builders* (Grove Press, N. Y., 1961), p. 95.

expressed an intensity of conviction never again reached by any passion, whether of religion, of loyalty, of patriotism, or of wealth; perhaps never even paralleled by any single economic effort, except in war. . . ."[1]

It is interesting to note, in connection with the leisure for the working class that is predicted to come in this century as a result of automation, that the medieval working class was not overburdened with work. Indeed, as Jean Gimpel writes, "it ought to be envied rather than pitied, for its leisure was magnificently organized by the authorities and absolutely free. It is not unlikely that the medieval laborer's leisure had a considerable influence on the cathedral crusade and the work of enlarging the churches. . . ." [2]

This deep popular movement, according to Henry Adams, "surprised the people of the time and the men who were its instruments." And it is likely that the next deep popular movement, which must come in our West before too long, will also surprise the men who are its instruments. It too will have its intellectuals, and its priests, its excesses, its regimentations, its horrors, and its great works in the service of an ideal.

A prediction of this sort is not very credible in our day when except for a handful of political reformers, no one puts a common ideal above personal values. The surrender of self-importance and individuality such as occurred during the building of the cathedrals does not on the surface look very likely, unless it were to be made under the aegis of

[1] Adams, *op. cit.,* p. 95.
[2] Gimpel, *op. cit.,* p. 49.

self-defense during war. Since wars are not continuous in most periods, even this kind of group effort is infrequent and moreover has a destructive backwash that leaves both victor and defeated more disrupted and centerless than they were before. Any other common cause but war or a temporary emergency is rare, especially in a money-centered and relatively prosperous society such as ours.

Yet there have been some short crusades since the Middle Ages. When property rights were endangered by unions in Italy and Germany after the first World War, a cause was whipped up — anti-communism — and it consumed the labor movement in its fire. The American Revolution begat many political reforms, but the intensity drained off after England was defeated. The ideas of the French Revolution did not survive intact as a center of faith after Napoleon's defeat, yet for a brief period men had submerged their individualities for an ideal. Political crusades have short intense lives. The movement of mankind, however, toward the pole of a religious faith is an entirely different phenomenon; it is a slow, massive process that may take centuries before it is completely accepted by individualistic men reluctant to yield up their hearts or their lives.

The surrender to love for one's family or other human beings is one of life's most rewarding experiences. It seems narrow in scope but it is an inkling of the kind of self-consuming that can occur when one surrenders the ego to a great social-religious movement such as Christianity or Mohammedism. This concept is now antipathetic to the western world, so long nurtured on the dogma of self-

148

aggrandizement, the dogma so necessary in the practice of capitalism. But as the capitalistic system decays, and wars in its defense become less and less feasible, men will become aware that a different sort of world is not only attractive but possible. Just as Christianity moved into the vacuum of unbelief in the post-Hellenic world, men with imaginative force and the strength of self-denial will move in with a new purpose and be followed gradually by more and more believers.

Art, for the first time now available to all, will have the leading role in the new worship. Biology, especially research into the nerve cells and the complexities of heredity, will be one of the scientific tools used to create more sensitive human creatures to carry on the species. This does not mean aiming toward a world entirely made up of aesthetes, but rather a world magnetized toward the pole of art and in search of the physical mutation that will gradually expand the human consciousness. It does mean, moreover, that the level on which the confusions and controversies of the world of action occur would be a little more reasonable, a little truer to man's best possibilities. Physical brutality has been somewhat mitigated by Christianity, but the cruelties of our day based on acquisitiveness can also be modified if the values of creativity and sensibility become paramount. Tensions and distortions will always occur, but the general level — the platform of strife — will be measurably raised. And devotion to art will fill not only the vacuum of unbelief, but also the vacuum of leisure that will soon become a reality, as the production of goods is more and more taken care of by machines.

149

Faith in the value of experiencing and creating meaningful aesthetic forms does not, as is believed in our mercantile
society, turn out hypersensitive people unfit for the world
of action and the full experience of living. This is a
misconception based on the false goals of capitalism and
on the paucity of magnanimous, full-bodied artists in our
time. The denigration of the profession has reduced its
quality. But there have always been and still are strong,
secure, and virile men among artists, and there would be
many more in a society that called for them. Once the man
who lifted the heaviest club was the success. In time the
muscular hero was replaced by the clever and the ruthless.
This was a necessary development in a world that needed
an enormous production of goods as well as the intellectual,
scientific push toward technocracy, just as the club-wielding
man was necessary when goods consisted of animals to be
killed. Both kinds of strength represented survival needs;
both are outmoded now. The new hero, the new strong
man will come from another impulse toward survival. Even
an astute businessman can sense this:

> *"Fortune's* boss, Henry Luce, forsees an age of
> introspection — as mankind reaches its material goals,
> he believes, men will think and talk more about the
> meaning of life and human destiny. Man may discover
> that his purpose now is to act as 'a collaborator with
> God, in the whole of evolution.' "[1]

As economic activity fades in importance and able men

[1] *N. Y. Post.*

150

seek some goal worthy of their energies, they will inevitably be drawn to participate in some humanistic cause. The pole around which they unite may be a belief that we can direct our own evolution through changing biologically the quality of our species. This would be no more startling than what happened in the eleventh and twelfth centuries when men united around the symbol of compassion that was so necessary to mitigate a barbaric and rigid society. To quote Henry Adams once more:

> "Their attachment to Mary rested on an instinct of self-preservation. They knew their own peril. If there was to be a future life, Mary was their only hope. She alone represented Love. The Trinity were, or was One, and could by the nature of its essence administer justice alone . . . in that law, no human weakness or error could exist. . . . There was no crack or cranny in the system through which human frailty could hope for escape. . . . Without Mary, man had no hope except in atheism, and for atheism the world was not ready."[1]

Science and philosophy have brought us in our western world to the brink of universal atheism. Again we know our own peril, created by science — the threat of complete, man-made annihilation from the sky. Again there is no crack or cranny for escape. Neither is there now any Virgin to save us; the only unseen power is our own power to save ourselves. This only is our hope. The power of the atomic bomb lends urgency to the need to replace the

[1] Adams, *op. cit.*, pp. 101-02.

world's disunity with some faith that will put the present gloomy conflict into perspective against the magnificent spectacle of the long ages of evolution. It should be clear that it is evil to risk the rich fruit of millions of years of development on such a paltry disagreement as the one that now endangers mankind.

Before long there must be a vital outcry that man's offspring, science, shall not be used to destroy him but used instead to extend the long evolution of life that far overshadows in importance any present controversy. It may take a new religion to stop the conflict — Christianity is obviously not enough. Such a new religion may be built around the belief that by expanding our consciousness we can find new powers within us and reach a higher reality, just as life has done in the past. Biology and art, given full scope, might supplant the concept of the survival of the fittest with the more forceful *creation* of the fittest; man would thus be extending God's work with his own efforts.

Evolution is still something of a mystery. Darwinists were so busy fighting challenges from the churches that they overdid their emphasis on the purely rational aspects. Teilhard de Chardin points out that human development violates the law of entropy and that this violation has never been adequately explained. A mystery remains in the fantastic surplus of our hearing power and our color sense. The germ plasm, apparently immune to changes in the environment of the organism, may yet be subject to mutations under very special circumstances and conditions. Do electrons permeate the germ plasm in rare cases when the body is in a receptive state? Do brain cells thicken through certain activities related to sensitivity? Recently Lancelot Law Whyte, in *Internal Factors in Evolution,* brings an entirely new factor into the old Darwinism, an exciting idea that may change the whole theory of mutation. In his "Preface" he writes:

> "This book is about a surprise: a biological idea which is in the air, for it has come to many minds during the last fifteen years, but is still so new and strange and so little understood that few have realized its far-reaching importance. It may prove to be one of the most fertile scientific ideas of the century. . . .
>
> The idea is that in addition to Darwinian selection another selective process has also played an important role in determining the evolution of the species. It is now being suggested that beside the well-established competitive selection of the 'synthetic' theory of evolution, an internal selection process acts directly on mutations, mainly at the molecular, chromosomal, and cellular levels, in terms not of struggle and competition but of the system's capacity for coordinated activity. The Darwinian criterion of fitness for external competition has to be supplemented by another: that of good internal coordination. Internal coadaptation is necessary as well as external adaptation. This new idea is *Darwin structured,* and thereby transformed into something different. For a directive agency has come into sight."[1]

A directive agency has come into sight. Though a cooler phraseology than Teilhard de Chardin's *"within* of the

[1] White, *op. cit.,* p. 14.

earth" or "*psychic* face of that portion of the stuff of the cosmos enclosed from the beginning of time within the narrow scope of the earth," [1] this is still scientific mysticism. It arouses associations with creative art, and provides perhaps a vague clue to the nature of the coordinating, directing power the artist feels within him, springing from deep levels, and which he transfers to his audience through his works. Both layman and scientist are on shaky, still intangible ground here. All that one can unequivocally say is that the accretion of art through the centuries represents the highest human coordination so far, and that the natural instinct toward art must have something to do with the furthering of our evolution.

Another clue to the relationship is that both art and evolution are concerned with the emergence of novelty. The energy behind art is not only coordinative and directive, it is also innovative. Each new style brought forth by a great artist is a mutation, as is each new religion. The human race grows more human through these mutations. The vitality of an epoch and the vitality of its art and religion have always been connected. At high points their leadership has been taken for granted. At low ebb of faith, when art becomes as sick as the population, still the great artifacts remain as a reservoir of creative energy.

The importance of the warm aesthetic sensibility cannot be underestimated as we make our next transition. In our time, for reasons already underscored, art is better at

[1] Chardin, *op. cit.*, pp. 71-2.

154

transforming reality than religion. To a few, the miracle of art has always been more important than the trans-figurations of religion, and sensibility an active factor in their lives. But now this factor can be spread and intensified through great numbers of people as we begin to be aware of the implications of the artistic process, and how it ties in with the miracle of evolution. With its help we have progressed blindly through the centuries, now our eyes are beginning to open.

Through the senses, the human mind achieved its complexity. Sensuosity of nerve cells finally brought matter into the dimension of what we call consciousness. Art operating on the consciousness and through the consciousness but never divorcing itself from the unconscious levels has been one of the crucial tools in making this journey from the mute to the articulate. It is still a crucial tool for the journey into further consciousness. Even more than the purely intellectual exercise of science, the aesthetic exercise pulls, stretches, shocks and revitalizes all the tiers and stages of our nerve material, and is what will undoubtedly lead us into another, still dimly apprehended psychic dimension.

Training for the full intake of art is as important as scientific research into the brain. The contemplation that is necessary — contemplation severed from motor response, self-aggrandizement, anxiety, ambition — could become a mystic experience not only for the few but for the many. One of the blessings of our mass culture is that so much of mankind is gradually being initiated into the world of sensitivity. The cries of alarm about kitsch and cheap popular entertainment is at base merely an attack on the society which is interested in profiteering from art. The potential of the modern audience has never been fairly estimated. Once again we see the economic obsession degrading men in a not too obvious but yet strident way. In a world where arts were worshipped, the whole society would be geared to raising the level of all, and in such an ambience greater works than have yet been dreamed of would appear. As we have seen, the stonemasons once produced magnificent art. Greatness comes from the spirit animating a time; and the paltry spirit of today produces paltry work. To blame this on the masses is to miss the point. It is on the shoulders of the masses, united in a new faith, that great art will be born again. And it will be for the first time not an accidental offshoot of religion but the very heart and center, the means, the voice of the faith.

The era may not be far off when deliberate training in art — both its creation and its reception — will be as extensive as the religious training the Church has made so effective for a thousand years. Such education could change the whole lives of children, whether or not they become artists themselves. A scientific approach to the group subconscious through the universal channels of art might save society from suicide. Only a few can devote themselves to outer space. But all can explore the new inner world of ideas and sensations waiting to be found in the human mind, and all can take a part in developing this other landscape of consciousness.

Intimations of the numinous function of art come from men who have devoted their lives to sensibility in all its phases and forms. Berenson writes of the "feeling of higher potency, fuller capacity, greater competence due to the sense of unexpected ease of our functions, induced by the arts of visual representation." [1] Donald Ferguson, in *Music and Metaphor* writes of the effect of a performance of Bach on an audience unfamiliar with classical music:

> ". . . there was an incredibly long interval of absolute silence: of that dumbfounded silence in which men contemplate a revelation. . . .
>
> It was with such a pang that we grasped the sense of Bach's music. Its tones and rhythms had indeed set forth no facts to build up our sensitivity to that meaning. But there was reference to experience, nevertheless — to experience dimly understood and variously comprehended by every hearer; and no 'purely' musical structure, seen without reference to that experience, could have assumed the dimensions of that pronouncement, gravid with meaning, which entered our minds with the stuff of that concert. We were aware of a knowable reality. . . . Somehow, this music spoke truth.
>
> The truth of which this music spoke had already presented itself to us — originally, no doubt, through the senses, but ultimately in terms not of physical but of spiritual experience. I have no hesitation in asserting that the experience itself was one which we call by such names as faith and ecstasy." [2]

[1] Bernard Berenson, *Aesthetics and History* (Pantheon Books, 1948), p. 152.

[2] Donald Ferguson, *Music and Metaphor* (University of Minnesota Press, 1960), pp. 9 and 16.

157

Plato felt a "sacred fear" of artists; art has been continually connected with "demonic" anarchy; its powers have been resisted and smothered as men needed to develop other, more worldly, less sensitive areas of consciousness in order to control their physical environment. But the persistence of this "sacred" instinct in man has kept his sensibility alive through the long slow process of unconscious evolution.

Conscious speeding up of evolution is not a fantastic concept nowadays. In his Foreword to the nineteen essays collected under the title of *Evolution as a Process,* Julian Huxley wrote:

> ". . . the final step of progress which produced man was solely concerned with improvements of the brain and its capacities, psychological and mental.
> The new phase of evolution thus opened up was characterized by a new relation between the organism and its environment. The human type became a microcosm which, through its capacities for awareness, was able to incorporate increasing amounts of the macrocosm into itself, to organize them in newer and richer ways, and then with their aid to exert new and more powerful influences on the macrocosm. And the present situation represents a further highly remarkable point in the development of our planet — the critical point at which the evolutionary process, as now embodied in man, has for the first time become aware of itself, is studying the laws of its own unfolding, and has a dawning realization of the possibilities of its future guidance or control. In other words, evolution

is on the verge of becoming internalized, conscious, and self-directing."[1]

The play has begun. It deals with man mutant, and with devotion to an idea that can call on his mysticism, his art, and his science. It can arouse his hope again and give him a new center of urgency. The future of mankind has spiritual possibilities outside the realm of present knowledge. To invade the new realm deliberately involves risks, but into it we must go. Man is too curious a creature to stop now. Blunders can lead to deterioration or extinction, yet to remain where we are, halfway to full humanity, is even more dangerous. The nearness of God is implicit in the reaching imagination, in the development of finer and finer sensibility. Christianity, a religion based on scarcity, suffering, and the consolations of a promised paradise after death, will give way to a faith in the perfectibility of life on this earth. Existence will gather a meaning far beyond physical or economic survival, which will be taken care of by ethical regulation of sex and technology. It is through the aesthetic brain, biologically based in form, feeling and language that we will lean toward God, toward the spirit that has animated the changes on earth up to this moment and that is working even now. For while religions die, their arts live on.

[1] Huxley, *op. cit.,* p. 23.

BIBLIOGRAPHY

Adams, Henry. *Mont-Saint-Michel and Chartres*. Houghton Mifflin, 1930.

Ayer, Alfred J. *Language, Truth and Logic*. Dover, 1953.

Beck, William S. *Modern Science and the Nature of Life*. Penguin, 1961.

Bonner, John Tyler. *The Ideas of Biology*. Harper & Row, 1962.

Carrington, Richard. *A Million Years of Man*. New American Library, 1964.

Cassirer, Ernst. *An Essay on Man*. Yale University Press, 1944.

———. *The Philosophy of Symbolic Forms*. Yale University Press, 1953.

Chardin, Pierre Teilhard de. *The Phenomenon of Man*. Harper & Row, Torchbooks, 1961.

Dobzhansky, Theodosius. *The Biology of Ultimate Concern*. New American Library, 1967.

Frank, Joseph. *The Widening Gyre*. Rutgers University Press, 1963.

Gimpel, Jean. *The Cathedral Builders*. Grove Press, 1961.

Gombrich, E. H. *Art and Illusion*. Bollingen Series, Pantheon Books, 1956.

———. *Meditations on a Hobby Horse*. Phaidon Press, 1963.

Hospers, John. *Meaning and Truth in the Arts*. Chapel Hill Books, 1946.

Huxley, Julian. *Evolution in Action*. Harper, 1953.

———(ed.). *Evolution as a Process*. Collier Books, 1963.

Jenkins, Iredell. *Art and the Human Enterprise*. Harvard University Press, 1953.

Koestler, Arthur. *The Act of Creation*. Macmillan, 1965.

Leepa, Allen. *The Challenge of Modern Art*. A. S. Barnes, 1957.

Malraux, André. *The Voices of Silence*. Pantheon Books, 1930.

Manuel, Frank. *Shapes of Philosophical History*. Stanford University Press, 1965.

Margolis, Joseph. *Philosophy Looks at the Arts*. Charles Scribner, 1962.

Mondrian, Pieter. *Plastic Art and Pure Plastic Art*. George Wittenborn, 1945.

Portmann, Adolph. *New Paths in Biology*. Harper & Row, 1964.

Rader, Melvin. *A Modern Book of Aesthetics*. Henry Holt, 1952.

Read, Herbert. *The Forms of Things Unknown*. Horizon Press, 1960.

——. *Icon and Idea*. Harvard University Press, 1955.

Rhodes, F. H. T. *The Evolution of Life*. Penguin Books, 1962.

Smith, G. Elliot. *The Evolution of Man*. Oxford University Press, 1924.

Sonneborn, T. M. (ed.). *The Control of Human Heredity and Evolution*. Macmillan, 1965.

Stace, W. T. *The Meaning of Beauty*. Richards & Toulmin, 1929.

Toulmin, Stephen and Goodfield, June. *The Architecture of Matter*. Penguin, 1965.

Walter, W. Grey. *The Living Brain*. Penguin, 1961.

Whyte, Lancelot Law. (ed.). *Aspects of Form*. Indiana University Press, 1961.

——. *The Internal Factors in Evolution*. George Braziller, 1965.

Williams, Hiram. *Notes for a Young Painter*. Prentice-Hall, 1963.

Wind, Edgar. *Art and Anarchy*. Faber & Faber, 1963.

Woodbridge, Dean E. *The Machinery of the Brain*. McGraw Hill, 1963.

Young, J. Z. *Doubt and Certainty in Science*. Oxford University Press, 1960.

W9-BYW-903

When Dreams Came True

When Dreams Came True

Classical Fairy Tales and Their Tradition

JACK ZIPES

ROUTLEDGE
New York and London

Published in 1999 by

Routledge
29 West 35th Street
New York, NY 10001

Published in Great Britain by

Routledge
11 New Fetter Lane
London EC4P 4EE

Printed in the United States of America on acid-free paper.
Text design by Jeff Hoffman.

Library of Congress Cataloging-in-Publication Data

Zipes, Jack David.
    When dreams came true: classical fairy tales and
  their tradition / Jack Zipes.
        p.   cm.
    Includes bibliographical references and index.
    ISBN 0-415-92150-3 (alk. paper). —
    ISBN 0-415-92151-1 (pbk.: alk. paper)
    1. Fairy tales—History and criticism.   I. Title.
    PN3437.Z57   1999
    398.21'09—DC21   98-6764
                                             CIP

For Catherine Mauger and Charlie Williams,
wonderful friends, who have helped some of my dreams come true in Paris

Contents

Preface

During the past twenty years the scholarship dealing with fairy tales has exploded, and we now have numerous enlightening studies about those mysterious tales that delight and haunt our lives from the cradle to death. We now have every conceivable approach, I think, that reflects how seriously we interpret and value fairy tales. Most recently Marina Warner has incisively explored the role women play as tellers and heroines of the tales in From the Beast to the Blonde: On Fairytales and Their Tellers (1994) to recuperate the significance of their contribution to the oral and literary tradition. Lewis Seifert has examined how fairy tales use the marvelous to mediate between conflicting cultural desires in Fairy Tales, Sexuality, and Gender in France 1690–1715: Nostalgic Utopias (1996). Philip Lewis has situated Charles Perrault in the literary and philosophical debates of the late seventeenth century in Seeing Through the Mother Goose Tales: Visual Turns in the Writings of Charles Perrault (1996) and demonstrated how Perrault reappropriated what was vital to institutionalizing culture in his fairy tales. Cristina Bacchilega has dealt with the question of gender and highly complex contemporary tales from a feminist viewpoint in Postmodern Fairy Tales: Gender and Narrative Strategies (1997). Nancy Canepa has edited a superb collection of essays in Out of the Woods: The Origins of the Literary Fairy Tale in Italy and France that lays the groundwork for a comprehensive history of the genre. U. C. Knoepflmacher has undertaken a psychological exploration of the constructions of childhood in Victorian fairy tales in Ventures into Childland: Victorians, Fairy Tales, and Femininity (1998) that were shaped by a common longing for a lost feminine complement. All six of these exceptional studies advance our knowledge of literary fairy tales, yet they leave many questions unanswered because we do not have a social history of the fairy tale within which to frame their findings.

My present study is a move in that direction. During the last fifteen years I have written approximately twelve introductions and afterwords to collections of fairy tales with an eye toward writing a social history of the literary fairy tale. My focus has been on the role that the literary fairy tale has assumed in the civilizing process by imparting values, norms, and aesthetic taste to children and adults. If the fairy tale is a literary genre, I have insisted that we try to grasp the sociogeneric and historical roots of the tales and investigate the manner in which particular authors used the genre of the fairy tale to articulate their personal desires, political views, and aesthetic preferences. The fairy tale has been historically determined and is overdetermined by writers with unusual talents and tantalizing views about their search for happiness which is coincidentally ours as well. The dramatic quality of the best fairy tales lies in the tension between the author's utopian longings and society's regulation of drives and desires.

It is my hope that in bringing together the diverse introductions and afterwords that I have written, I can provide a sociohistorical framework for the study of the classical tradition of the literary fairy tale in Western society. I make no claims for complete coverage of the classical fairy tales, but I do try to deal with the most significant writers and their works in Europe and North America from the sixteenth century to the beginning of the twentieth century. And I do try to raise questions and provide partial answers to the sociocultural web woven by fairy-tale writers and the ramifications of this web for our use and abuse of fairy tales today. Most of the scholarship that I have used in writing this book will be apparent in my text. Therefore, I have decided to forgo footnotes in this work. Readers may consult the bibliography for further study. I have listed the sources of my own essays at the end of the bibliography. All of the essays have been revised and brought up to date with respect to details important for drafting a social and literary history.

As usual, I should like to thank Bill Germano, who prods me with magical ideas and has been most supportive in all my endeavors at Routledge. Lai Moy has done a great job in managing the production of my book, and I am very grateful to Alexandria Giardino for the careful and thorough copyediting of this volume.

Jack Zipes
June 1998

one

Spells of Enchantment

An Overview of the History of Fairy Tales

It has generally been assumed that fairy tales were first created for children and are largely the domain of children. Nothing could be further from the truth.

From the very beginning, thousands of years ago, when tales were told to create communal bonds in the face of inexplicable forces of nature, to the present, when fairy tales are written and told to provide hope in a world seemingly on the brink of catastrophe, mature men and women have been the creators and cultivators of the fairy-tale tradition. When introduced to fairy tales, children welcome them mainly because the stories nurture their great desire for change and independence. On the whole, the literary fairy tale has become an established genre within a process of Western civilization that cuts across all ages. Even though numerous critics and shamans have mystified and misinterpreted the fairy tale because of their spiritual quest for universal archetypes or need to save the world through therapy, both the oral and literary forms of the fairy tale are grounded in history: they emanate from specific struggles to humanize bestial and barbaric forces, which have terrorized our minds and communities in concrete ways, threatening to destroy free will and human compassion. The fairy tale sets out to conquer this concrete terror through metaphors.

Though it is difficult to determine when the first *literary* fairy tale was conceived and extremely difficult to define exactly what a fairy tale is, we do know that oral folk tales, which contain wondrous and marvelous elements, have existed for thousands of years and were told largely by adults for adults. Motifs from these tales, which were memorized and passed on by word of mouth, made their way into the Bible and the Greek classics such as *The Iliad* and *The Odyssey*. The early oral tales which served as the basis for the development of literary fairy tales were closely tied to the rituals, customs, and beliefs of tribes, communities, and trades. They fostered a sense of belonging and hope that miracles involving some kind of magical transformation were possible to bring about a better world. They instructed, amused, warned, initiated, and enlightened. They opened windows to imaginative worlds inside that needed concrete expression outside in reality. They were to be shared and exchanged, used and modified according to the needs of the tellers and the listeners.

Tales are marks that leave traces of the human struggle for immortality. Tales are human marks invested with desire. They are formed like musical notes of compositions except that the letters constitute words and are chosen individually to enunciate the speaker/writer's position in the world, including his or her dreams, needs, wishes, and experiences. The speaker/writer posits the self against language to establish identity and to test the self with and against language. Each word marks a way toward a future different from what may have been decreed, certainly different from what is being experienced in the present: The words that are selected in the process of creating a tale allow the speaker/writer freedom to play with options that no one has ever glimpsed. The marks are magical.

The fairy tale celebrates the marks as magical: marks as letters, words, sentences, signs. More than any other literary genre, the fairy tale has persisted in emphasizing transformation of the marks with spells, enchantments, disenchantments, resurrections, recreations. During its inception, the fairy tale distinguished itself as genre both by appropriating the oral folk tale and expanding it, for it became gradually necessary in the modern world to adapt the oral tale to standards of literacy and to make it acceptable for diffusion in the public sphere. The fairy tale is only one type of appropriation of a particular oral storytelling tradition: the wonder folk tale, often called the *Zaubermärchen* or the *conte merveilleux*. As more and more wonder tales were written down in the fifteenth, sixteenth, and seventeenth centuries, they constituted the genre of the literary fairy tale that began establishing its own conventions, motifs, topoi, characters, and plots, based to a large extent on those developed in the oral tradition but altered to address a reading public formed by the aristocracy and the middle classes. Though the peasants were excluded in the formation of this literary tradition, it was their material, tone, style, and beliefs that were incorporated into the new genre in the fifteenth, sixteenth, and seventeenth centuries.

What exactly is the oral wonder tale?

In Vladimir Propp's now famous study, *The Morphology of the Folk Tale* (1968), he outlined thirty-one basic functions that constitute the formation of a paradigm, which was and still is common in Europe and North America. By functions, Propp meant the fundamental and constant components of a tale that are the acts of a character and necessary for driving the action forward. To summarize the functions with a different emphasis:

1. The protagonist is confronted with an interdiction or prohibition that he or she violates in some way.

2. Departure or banishment of the protagonist, who is either given a task or assumes a task related to the interdiction of prohibition. The protagonist is *assigned* a task, and the task is a *sign*. That is, his or her character will be marked by the task that is his or her sign.

3. Encounter with (a) villain; (b) mysterious individual or creature, who gives the protagonist gifts; (c) three different animals or creatures who are helped by the protagonist and promise to repay him or her; (d) encounter with three different animals or creatures who offer gifts to help the protagonist, who is in trouble. The gifts are often magical agents, which bring about miraculous change.

4. The endowed protagonist is tested and moves on to battle and conquer the villain or inimical forces.

5. The peripety or sudden fall in the protagonist's fortunes that is generally only a temporary setback. A wonder or miracle is needed to reverse the wheel of fortune.

6. The protagonist makes use of endowed gifts (and this includes the magical agents and cunning) to achieve his or her goal. The result is (a) three battles with the villain; (b) three impossible tasks that are nevertheless made possible; (c) the breaking of a magic spell.

7. The villain is punished or the inimical forces are vanquished.

8. The success of the protagonist usually leads to (a) marriage; (b) the acquisition of money; (c) survival and wisdom; (d) any combination of the first three.

Rarely do wonder tales end unhappily. They triumph over death. The tale begins with "once upon a time" or "once there was" and never really ends when it ends. The ending is actually the true beginning. The once upon a time is not a past designation but futuristic: the timelessness of the tale and lack of geographical specificity endow it with utopian connotations — utopia in its original meaning designated "no place," a place that no one had ever envisaged. We form and keep the utopian kernel of the tale safe in our imaginations with hope.

The significance of the paradigmatic functions of the wonder tale is that they facilitate recall for teller and listeners. They enable us to store, remember, and reproduce the utopian spirit of the tale and to change it to fit our experiences and desires due to the easily identifiable characters who are associated with particular assignments and settings. For instance, we have the simpleton who turns out to be remarkably cunning; the third and youngest son who is oppressed by his brothers and/or father; the beautiful but maltreated youngest daughter; the discharged soldier who has been exploited by his superiors; the shrew who needs taming; the evil witch; the kind elves; the cannibalistic ogre; the clumsy stupid giant; terrifying beasts like dragons, lions, and wild boars; kind animals like ants, birds, deer, bees, ducks, and fish; the clever tailor; the evil and jealous stepmother; the clever peasant; the power-hungry and unjust king; treacherous nixies; the beast-bridegroom. There are haunted castles; enchanted forests; mysterious huts in woods; glass mountains; dark, dangerous caves; underground kingdoms. There are seven-league boots that enable the protagonist to move faster than jet planes; capes that make a person invisible; magic wands that can perform extraordinary feats of transformation; animals that produce gold; tables that provide all the delicious and sumptuous food you can eat; musical instruments with enormous captivating powers; swords and clubs capable of conquering anyone or anything; lakes, ponds, and seas that are difficult to cross and serve as the home for supernatural creatures.

The characters, settings, and motifs are combined and varied according to specific functions to induce *wonder*. It is this sense of wonder that distinguished the wonder tales from other oral tales such as the legend, the fable, the anecdote, and the myth; it is clearly the sense of wonder that distinguishes the *literary* fairy tale from the moral story, novella, sentimental tale, and other modern short literary genres. Wonder causes astonishment. As marvelous object or phenomenon, it is often regarded as a supernatural occurrence and can be an omen or portent. It gives rise to admiration, fear, awe, and reverence. The *Oxford Universal Dictionary* states that wonder is "the emotion excited by the perception of something novel and unexpected, or inexplicable; astonishment mingled with perplexity or bewildered curiosity." In the oral wonder tale, we are to wonder about the workings of the universe where anything can happen at any time, and these happy or fortuitous events are never to be explained. Nor do the characters demand an explanation — they are opportunistic. They are encouraged to be so, and if they do not take advantage of the opportunity that will benefit them in their relations with others, they are either dumb or mean-spirited. The tales seek to awaken our regard for the miraculous condition of life and to evoke in a religious sense profound feelings of awe and respect for life as a miraculous process, which can be altered and changed to compensate for the lack of power, wealth, and pleasure that most people experience. Lack, deprivation, prohibition, and interdiction motivate people to look for signs of fulfillment and emancipation. In the wonder tales, those who are naive and simple are able to succeed because they are untainted and can recognize the wondrous signs. They have retained their belief in the miraculous condition of nature, revere nature in all its aspects. They have not been spoiled by conventionalism, power, or rationalism. In contrast to the humble characters, the villains are those who use words intentionally to exploit, control, transfix, incarcerate, and destroy for their benefit. They have no respect or consideration for nature and other human beings, and they actually seek to abuse magic by preventing change and causing everything to be transfixed according to their interests. Enchantment = petrification. Breaking the spell = emancipation. The wondrous protagonist wants to keep the process of natural change flowing and indicates possibilities for overcoming the obstacles that prevent other characters or creatures from living in a peaceful and pleasurable way.

The focus on wonder in the oral folk tale does not mean that all wonder tales, and later the literary fairy tales, served and serve an emancipatory purpose. The nature and meaning of folk tales have depended on the stage of development of a tribe, community, or society. Oral tales have served to stabilize, conserve, or challenge the common beliefs, laws, values, and norms of a group. The ideology expressed in wonder tales always stemmed from the position that the narrator assumed with regard to the developments in his or her community, and the narrative plot and changes made in it depended on the sense of wonder or awe that the narrator wanted to evoke. In other words, the sense of wonder in the tale and the intended emotion sought by the narrator is ideological.

Since these wonder tales have been with us for thousands of years and have undergone so many different changes in the oral tradition, it is difficult to determine the ideological intention of the narrator. When we disregard the narrator's intention, it is often difficult to reconstruct (and/or deconstruct) the ideological meaning of a tale. In the last analysis, however, even if we cannot establish whether a wonder tale is ideologically conservative, sexist, progressive, emancipatory, and so forth, it is the celebration of wonder that accounts for its major appeal. No matter what the plot may be, this type of tale calls forth our capacity as readers and potential transmitters of its signs and meanings to wonder. We do not want to know the exact resolution, the "happily ever after," of a tale, that is, what it is actually like. We do not want to name God, gods, goddesses, or fairies, who will forever remain mysterious and omnipotent. We do not want to form craven images. We do not want utopia designated for us. We want to remain curious, startled, provoked, mystified, and uplifted. We want to glare, gaze, gawk, behold, and stare. We want to be given opportunities to change. Ultimately we want to be told that we can become kings and queens, or lords of our own destinies. We remember wonder tales and fairy tales to keep our sense of wonderment alive and to nurture our hope that we can seize possibilities and opportunities to transform ourselves and our worlds.

Ultimately, the definition of both the wonder tale and the fairy tale, which derives from it, depends on the manner in which a narrator/ author arranges *known* functions of a tale aesthetically and ideologically to induce wonder and then transmits the tale as a whole according to customary usage of a society in a given historical period. The first stage for the literary fairy tale involved a kind of class and perhaps even gender appropriation. The voices of the nonliterate tellers were submerged, and since women in most cases were not allowed to be scribes, the tales were scripted according to male dictates or fantasies, even though they may have been told by women. Put crudely, one could say that the literary appropriation of the oral wonder tales served the hegemonic interests of males within the upper classes of particular communities and societies, and to a great extent, this is true. However, such a crude statement must be qualified, for the writing down of the tales also preserved a great deal of the value system of those deprived of power. The more the literary fairy tale was cultivated and developed, the more it became individualized and varied by intellectuals and artists, who often sympathized with the marginalized in society or were marginalized themselves. The literary fairy tale allowed for new possibilities of subversion in the written word and in print; therefore it was always looked upon with misgivings by the governing authorities in the civilization process.

During early Christianity there were not many signs that the oral folk tales would develop and flourish as a major literary genre in the West, and there were obvious reasons for this lack: Most people were nonliterate and shared strong oral cultural traditions; the tales had not been changed sufficiently to serve the taste and interests of the ruling classes; Latin was the dominant intellectual and literary language until the late Middle Ages when the vernacular languages gradually formed general standards of grammar and orthography for communication; the technology of printing did not make much progress until the fifteenth century so that the distribution of literary works was not very widespread. Consequently, it is not surprising that the first appearance of a major literary fairy tale, Apuleius's "Psyche and Cupid," was in Latin and came in the second century. Moreover, it was included in a book, *The Golden Ass*, which dealt with metamorphoses, perhaps the key theme of the fairy tale up to the present. However, whereas many oral wonder tales had been concerned with the humanization of natural forces, the literary fairy tale, beginning with "Psyche and Cupid," shifted the emphasis more toward the civilization of the protagonist who must learn to respect particular codes and laws to become accepted in society and/or united to reproduce and continue the progress of the world toward perfect happiness.

At first, this new literary fairy tale could not stand by itself, that is, it did not have a receptive audience and had to be included within a frame story or in a collection of instructive and amusing stories and anecdotes. Therefore, up to the fifteenth century, the only other evidence we have of complete fairy tales are within such manuscripts as the *Gesta Romanorum* (c.1300), medieval romances, or in sermons delivered by priests. Fairy tales like "Of Feminine Subtlety" in the *Gesta Romanorum* were generally used to provide instruction for the education of young Christian boys and had a strong moralistic strain to them. In addition, like "Cupid and Psyche," the early Latin fairy tales were largely addressed to the male sex and focused on their acquisition of the proper moral values and ethics that would serve them in their positions of power in society.

It was not until the publication of Giovan Francesco Straparola's *Le piacevoli notti* (*The Pleasant Nights*) in 1550–1553 that fairy tales were first published in the vernacular and for a mixed audience of upperclass men and women (fig. 1). Straparola brings together a group of aristocrats who flee Milan for political reasons and decide to tell tales to one another to amuse themselves during their exile. The frame narrative is set up to include erotic anecdotes, fables, and fairy tales like "The Pig Prince" and "Constantino," forerunners of "Hans My Hedgehog" and "Puss in Boots," and it is modeled after Boccacio's

Figure 1. "The Pig Prince." From Giovan Francesco Straparola's *The Facetious Nights*. Trans. William G. Waters. Illustr. E. R. Hughes. London: Lawrence & Bullen, 1894.

The Decameron. However, Boccaccio did not include fairy tales in his collection so that Straparola can be considered the first writer in Europe to have published fairy tales in the vernacular for an educated audience. Though his tales did not achieve the popularity of Boccaccio's collection, they were reprinted several times in Italian during the next few centuries and, by the nineteenth century, were translated into French, German, and English.

There is no direct evidence, however, one way or the other that Straparola influenced Giambattista Basile, whose *Lo Cunto de li Cunti*, also known as *The Pentameron*, was published posthumously in 1634. Written in Neapolitan dialect, Basile was the first writer to use an old folk-tale motif about laughter to frame an entire collection of fifty fairy tales. His book begins with a tale about a princess named Zoza who cannot laugh, no matter what her father, the King of Vallepelosa, does to try to assuage her melancholy. Finally, her father orders that a fountain of oil be erected before the palace gate so that people would skip and jump to avoid being soiled. Thereby, the king hoped that his daughter would laugh at the stumbling people and overcome her melancholy. Indeed, the princess does laugh but at the wrong person, an old witch of a woman, who places a curse on her and declares that if Zoza is ever to marry it must be to Taddeo, a bewitched sleeping prince, whom only she can wake and save with her tears. With the help and advice from three fairies, Zoza succeeds in weeping a sufficient amount of tears, but she then falls asleep before she can achieve the honor of rescuing Taddeo. In the meantime, a malicious slave steals her vessel of tears and claims the honor of liberating Taddeo, who marries her. Yet, this does not deter Zoza, who rents a fine house opposite Taddeo's palace and manages through her beauty to attract his attention. Once the slave, who is pregnant, learns about this, she threatens to kill the child in her stomach if Taddeo does not obey her every whim. Zoza responds by enticing the slave with three gifts that she had received from the fairies. The third one is a doll that makes the slave addicted to fairy tales, and she forces Taddeo to gather storytellers, who will amuse her during the final ten days of her pregnancy. So, Taddeo gathers a group of ten motley women, who tell five fairy tales a day until Zoza concludes the sessions with her own tale that exposes the slave's theft and brings the frame story to its conclusion. As a result, Taddeo has the pregnant slave put to death and takes Zoza for his new wife.

Basile was very familiar with the customs and behavior of the Neapolitans and had also traveled widely in Italy and served at different courts. Therefore, he was able to include a wealth of folklore, anecdotes, and events in his fairy tales that celebrate miraculous changes and communion. A good example is "The Merchant's Two Sons," which has many different folk and literary versions. As in the frame narrative, the humane ties between people based on compassion and love can only be solidified if the protagonists recognize what and where evil is. The fairy tale involves arousing the protagonists and sharpening their perception of what is really occurring so that they can change or bring about changes to master their own destinies. In this respect, the narrative structure of the fairy tale is conceived so that the listener will learn to distinguish between destructive and beneficial forces, for the art of seeing and intuiting is nurtured by the fairy tale.

It is not by chance that the literary fairy tale began flourishing in Italy before other European countries. During the fifteenth and sixteenth centuries, the Italian cities and duchies had prospered by developing great commercial centers, and the literacy rate had grown immensely. Cultural activity at the courts and in the city-states was high, and there was a great deal of foreign influence on storytelling as well as strong native oral traditions among the people. Although it cannot be fully documented, it is highly likely that the Italian literary fairy tales were gradually spread in print and by word of mouth throughout Europe. Interestingly, England, another powerful maritime country, was the other nation that began cultivating a literary fairy-tale tradition. There are fairy-tale elements in Chaucer's *The Canterbury Tales* (c. 1386–1400), in Spenser's *The Faerie Queen* (1590–96), and, of course, in many of Shakepeare's plays such as *King Lear*, *A Midsummer Night's Eve*, *The Taming of the Shrew*, and *The Tempest*, all written between 1590 and 1611. However, due to the Puritan hostility toward amusement during the seventeenth century, the fairy tale as a genre was not able to flourish in England. Instead, the genre had more propitious conditions in France and virtually bloomed in full force toward the end of the ancien régime from 1690 to 1714.

There were many contributing factors that account for the rise and spread of the fairy tale in France at this time. First of all, France had become the most powerful country in Europe and the French language, considered to be the most cultivated, was used at most courts throughout all of Europe. Secondly, the evolution of printing favored more experimentation of different kinds of literature. Thirdly, there was great cultural creativity and innovation in France. Finally, about the middle of the seventeenth century, the fairy tale gradually became more accepted at literary salons and at the court particularly in theatrical form. Fairy-tale recitations and games were devised, generally by women in their salons, and they eventually led to the publication of the fairy tales during the 1790s. Perhaps the most prodigious (and also most prolific) of the French fairy-tale writers was Mme Marie-Catherine D'Aulnoy, whose first tale, "The Island of Happiness," was embedded in her novel *Histoire d'Hippolyte, comte de Duglas* (1790). However, it was not until she had established a popular literary salon, in which fairy tales were regularly presented, that she herself published four volumes of fairy tales between 1696 and 1698. Though Charles Perrault is generally considered to be the most significant French writer of fairy tales of this period, Mme D'Aulnoy was undoubtedly more typical and more of a catalyst for other writers. Her narratives are long and rambling and focus on the question of *tendresse*, that is, true and natural feelings between a man and a woman, whose nobility will depend on their manners and the ways they uphold standards of civility in defending their love. "Green Serpent" is a good example of Mme D'Aulnoy's concerns and shows how she was influenced by Apuleius's "Cupid and Psyche" and was familiar with the Italian tradition of fairy tales, not to mention French folklore. In turn her fairy tales set the stage for the works of Mlle L'Héritier, whose "Ricdin-Ricdon" (1696) is a remarkable courtly interpretation of "Rumpelstiltskin," and Mlle de la Force, whose "Parslinette" (1697) is a fascinating version of "Rapunzel." Of course, the writer, whose name has become practically synonymous with term *conte de fée* (fairy tale) is Charles Perrault, who wrote two verse tales "The Foolish Wishes" (1693) and

"Donkey Skin" (1694) and then published the famous prose renditions of "Cinderella," "Little Red Riding Hood," "Sleeping Beauty," "Blue Beard," "Tom Thumb," "Rickey with the Tuft," and "The Fairies" in *Histoires ou contes du temps passé* (1697). Perrault, who frequented the literary salons in Paris, purposely sought to establish the literary fairy tale as an innovative genre that exemplified a modern sensibility that was coming into its own and was to be equated with the greatness of French *civilité*. Not all the French writers of this period intended to celebrate the splendor of the ancien régime, but they all were concerned with questions of manners, norms, and mores in their tales and sought to illustrate proper behavior and what constituted noble feelings in their narratives. Almost all the writers lived in Paris, where their tales were published. Therefore, the "mode" of writing fairy tales was concentrated within a feudal sphere and led to what could be called the institutionalization of the genre, for after the appearance of *The Thousand and One Nights* (1704–17) in ten volumes translated and adapted into French by Antoine Galland, the literary fairy tale became an acceptable, social-symbolic form through which conventionalized motifs, characters, and plots were selected, composed, arranged, and rearranged to comment on the civilizing process and to keep alive the possibility of miraculous change and a sense of wonderment.

The very name of the genre itself — *fairy tale* — originated during this time, for the French writers coined the term *conte de fée* during the seventeenth century, and it has stuck to the genre in Europe and North America ever since. This "imprint" is important because it reveals something crucial about the fairy tale that has remained part of its nature to the present. The early writers of fairy tales placed the power of metamorphosis in the hands of women — the redoubtable fairies. In addition, this miraculous power was not associated with a particular religion or mythology through which the world was to be explained. It was a secular mysterious power of compassion that could not be explained, and it derived from the creative imagination of the writer. Anyone could call upon the fairies for help. It is clear that the gifted French women writers at the seventeenth century preferred to address themselves to a fairy and to have a fairy resolve the conflicts in their fairy tales than the Church with its male-dominated hierarchy.

After all, it was the Church, which had eliminated hundreds of thousands of so-called female witches during the previous two centuries in an effort to curb heretical and nonconformist beliefs. However, those "pagan" notions survived in the tradition of the oral wonder tale and surfaced again in published form in France when it became safer to introduce other supernatural powers and creatures in a symbolical code than those officially sanctioned by the Christian code. In short, there was something subversive about the institutionalization of the fairy tale in France during the 1790s, for it enabled writers to create a dialogue about norms, manners, and power that evaded court censorship and freed the fantasy of the writers and readers, while at the same time paying tribute to the French code of *civilité* and the majesty of the aristocracy. Once certain discursive paradigms and conventions were established, a writer could demonstrate his or her "genius" by rearranging, expanding, deepening, and playing with the known functions of a genre, which, by 1715, had already formed a type of canon that consisted not only of the great classical tales such as "Cinderella," "Sleeping Beauty," "Rapunzel," "Rumpelstiltskin," "Puss in Boots," "Little Red Riding Hood," "Beauty and the Beast," "Bluebeard," "The Golden Dwarf," "The Blue Bird," and "The White Cat," but also the mammoth collection of *The Arabian Nights*.

Galland's project of translating the Arabic tales from original manuscripts, which stemmed from the fourteenth century and were based on an oral tradition, was important for various reasons: His translation was not literal, and he introduced many changes influenced by French culture into his adaptations; eight of the tales, one of which was "Prince Ahmed and the Fairy Pari-Banou," were obtained from a Maronite Christian scholar named Youhenna Diab, living at that time in Paris, and were in part Galland's literary re-creations. The exotic setting and nature of these Oriental tales attracted not only French but numerous European readers so that Galland's translation stimulated the translation of other Arabic works such as *The Adventures of Abdalah, Son of Anif* (1712–14) by the abbot Jean-Paul Bignon and hundreds of his own translations into English, Italian, German, Spanish, and so on.

The infusion of the Oriental tales into the French literary tradition enriched and broadened the paradigmatic options for Western writers during the course of the eighteenth century. It became a favorite device (and still is) to deploy the action of a tale to the Orient while discussing sensitive issues of norms and power close to home. Aside from the great impact of the Arabic and Persian tales on Western writers through translations, there was another development that was crucial for the institutionalization of the fairy tale in the eighteenth century. Soon after the publication of the tales by D'Aulnoy, Perrault, L'Héritier, Galland, and others, they were reprinted in a series of chapbooks called the *Bibliothèque Bleue*, inexpensive volumes distributed by peddlers called *colporteurs* throughout France and central Europe to the lower classes. The fairy tales were often abridged; the language was changed and made more simple; and there were multiple versions, which were read to children and nonliterates. Many of these tales were then appropriated by oral storytellers so that the literary tradition became a source for the oral tradition. As a result of the increased popularity of the literary fairy tale as chapbook, which had first been prepared by the acceptance of the genre at court, the literary fairy tale for children began to be cultivated. Already during the 1690s, Fénelon, the important theologian and Archbishop of Cambrai who had been in charge of the Dauphin's education, had written several didactic fairy tales as an experiment to make the Dauphin's lessons more enjoyable. However, they were not considered proper and useful enough for the grooming of children from the upper classes to be published. They were first printed after his death in 1730; from that point on it became more acceptable to write and publish fairy tales for children just as long as they indoctrinated children according to gender-specific roles and class codes in the civilizing process. The most notable example here, aside from Fénelon's tales, is the voluminous work of Madame Le Prince de Beaumont, who published *Magasin des Enfants* (1756), which included "Beauty and the Beast," "Prince Chéri," and other overtly moralistic tales for children. Mme de Beaumont used a frame story to transmit different kinds of didactic tales in which a governess engaged several young girls between six and ten in discussions about morals, manners, ethics, and gender roles that lead her to tell stories to illustrate her points. Her utilization of such a frame was actually based on her work as a governess in England, and the frame was set up to be

copied by other adults to institutionalize a type of storytelling in
homes of the upper classes. It was only as part of the civilizing process
that storytelling developed within the aristocratic and bourgeois
homes in the seventeenth and eighteenth centuries, first through governesses and nannies and later in the eighteenth and nineteenth centuries through mothers who told good-night stories.

As the literary fairy tale now spread in France to every age group
and to every social class, it began to serve different functions, depending on the writer's interests: (1) representation of the glory and ideology of the French aristocracy; (2) symbolical critique of the
aristocratic hierarchy with utopian connotations, largely within the
aristocracy from the female viewpoint; (3) introduction of the norms
and values of the bourgeois civilizing process as more reasonable and
egalitarian than the feudal code; (4) amusement for the aristocracy
and bourgeoisie, whereby the fairy tale was a *divertissement*; it diverted
the attention of listeners/readers from the serious sociopolitical problems of the times; it compensated for the deprivation that the upper
classes perceived themselves to be suffering; (5) self-parody — to
reveal the ridiculous notions in previous fairy tales and to represent
another aspect of court society to itself; such parodies can be seen in
Jean-Jacques Cazotte's "A Thousand and One Follies" (1742), Jean-
Jacques Rousseau's "The Queen Fantasque" (1758), and Voltaire's
"The White Bull" (1774); and (6) careful cultivation of the literary
genre for children. Fairy tales with clear didactic and moral lessons
were finally approved as reading matter to serve as a subtle, more pleasurable means of initiating children into the class rituals and customs
that reinforced the status quo.

The climax of the French institutionalization of the fairy tale was
the publication of Charles Mayer's forty-one-volume *Le Cabinet des
Fées* between 1785 and 1789, a collection that included most of the
important French tales written during the previous hundred years.
From this point on, most writers, whether they wrote for adults or children, consciously held a dialogue with a fairy-tale discourse that had
become firmly established in the Western intellectual tradition. For
instance, the French fairy tale, which, we must remember, now
included *The Arabian Nights*, had a profound influence on the German

classicists and the romantics, and the development in Germany provided the continuity for the institution of the genre in the West as a
whole. Like the French authors, the German middle-class writers like
Johann Karl Musäus in his collection *Volksmärchen der Deutschen*
(1782–86), which included "Libussa," began employing the fairy tale
to celebrate German customs. Musäus combined elements of German
folklore and the French fairy tale in his work in a language clearly
addressed to educated Germans. At the same time, Christoph Martin
Wieland translated and adapted numerous tales from the *Cabinet des
Fées* in *Dschinnistan* (1786–87). "The Philosopher's Stone" is his own
creation but reveals how he, too, consciously used the fairy tale to portray the decadence of German feudal society and introduced Oriental
motifs to enhance its exoticism and to conceal his critique of his own
society. Aside from these two collections for upper-class readers,
numerous French fairy tales became known in Germany by the turn of
the century through the popular series of the *Blaue Bibliothek* and other
translations from the French. In fact, some like "Sleeping Beauty,"
"Cinderella," and "Little Red Riding Hood" even worked their way
into the Brothers Grimm collection of the *Kinder- und Hausmärchen*
(*Children's and Household Tales*, 1812–15), which were considered to
be genuinely German. Romantic writers such as Wilhelm Heinrich
Wackenroder, Ludwig Tieck, Novalis, Joseph von Eichendorff,
Clemens Brentano, Adelbert Chamisso, Friedrich de la Motte Fouqué,
and E. T. A. Hoffmann wrote extraordinary tales that revealed a major
shift in the function of the genre: the fairy tale no longer represented
the dominant aristocratic ideology. Rather, it was written as a critique
of the worst aspects of the enlightenment and absolutism. This viewpoint was clearly expressed in Johann Wolfgang Goethe's classical narrative simply entitled "The Fairy Tale" (1795) as though it were to be
the fairy tale to end all fairy tales. Goethe optimistically envisioned a
successful rebirth of a rejuvenated monarchy that enjoyed the support
of all social classes in his answer to the chaos and destruction of the
French Revolution. In contrast, the romantics were generally more
skeptical about the prospects for individual autonomy, the reform of
decadent institutions, and a democratic public sphere in a Germany,
divided by the selfish interests of petty tyrants and the Napoleonic

Wars. Very few of the German romantic tales end on a happy note. The protagonists either go insane or die. The evil forces assume a social hue, for the witches and villains are no longer allegorical representations of evil in the Christian tradition but are symbolically associated with the philistine bourgeois society or the decadent aristocracy. Nor was the purpose of the romantic fairy tale to amuse in the traditional sense of divertissement. Instead, it sought to engage the reader in a serious discourse about art, philosophy, education, and love. It is not by chance that the German term for the literary fairy tale is *Kunstmärchen* (art tale), for the utopian impulse for a better future was often carried on by an artist or a creative protagonist in the romantic narratives, and his fate indicated to what extent the civilizing process in Germany inhibited or nurtured the creative and independent development of the citizens.

While the function of the fairy tale for adults underwent a major shift — and this was clear in other countries as well — that made it an appropriate means to maintain a dialogue about social and political issues within the bourgeois public sphere, the fairy tale for children remained suspect until the 1820s. Although there were various collections published for children in the latter part of the eighteenth century and at the turn of the century along with individual chapbooks containing "Cinderella," "Jack the Giant Killer," "Beauty and the Beast," "Little Red Riding Hood," "Sleeping Beauty (fig. 2)," they were not regarded as the prime reading material for children. Nor were they considered to be "healthy" for the development of children's minds and bodies. In Germany, for instance, there was a debate about *Lesesucht* (obsessional reading) that could lead children to have crazy ideas and to masturbate. The stories considered most detrimental to the well-being of children were fantasy works. For the most part, the church leaders and educators favored other genres of stories — more realistic, sentimental, didactic — which were intended to demonstrate what good manners and morals were. Even the Brothers Grimm, in particular Wilhelm, began in 1819 to revise their collected tales, targeting them more for children than they had done in the beginning and cleansing their narratives of erotic, cruel, or bawdy passages. However, the fantastic and wondrous elements were kept so that they were

Figure 2. "Sleeping Beauty." From *Household Stories Collected by the Brothers Grimm*. Illustr. E. H. Wehnert. London: Routledge, c. 1900.

not at first fully accepted by the bourgeois reading public, which only began changing its attitude toward the fairy tale for children during the course of the 1820s and 1830s throughout Europe. It was signaled in Germany by the publication of Wilhelm Hauff's *Märchen Almanach* (1826), which contained "The Story of Little Muck," and in England by Edward Taylor's translation of the Grimms's *Kinder- und Hausmärchen* under the title of *German Popular Stories* (1823) with illustrations by the famous George Cruikshank. The reason for the more tolerant acceptance of the literary fairy tale for children may be attributed to the realization on the part of educators and parents, probably due to their own reading experiences, that fantasy literature and amusement would not necessarily destroy or pervert children's minds. Whether the children were of the middle classes and attended school, or were of the lower classes and worked on the farm or in a factory, they needed a recreation period — the time and space to re-create themselves without having morals and ethics imposed on them, without having the feeling that their reading or listening had to involve indoctrination.

Significantly it was from 1830 to 1900, during the rise of the middle classes, that the fairy tale came into its own for children. It was exactly during this time, from 1835 onward, to be precise, that Hans Christian Andersen, greatly influenced by the German romantic writers and the Grimms, began publishing his tales that became extremely popular throughout Europe and America. Andersen combined humor, Christian sentiments, and fantastic plots to form tales, which amused and instructed young and old readers at the same time. More than any writer of the nineteenth century, he fully developed what Perrault had begun: to write tales such as "The Red Shoes," which could be readily grasped by children and adults alike but with a different understanding. Some of his narratives like "The Shadow" were clearly intended for adults alone, and it is a good example of his use of the doppelgänger motif, developed by E. T. A. Hoffmann, and his exploration of paranoia within the fairy-tale genre to express his individual and very peculiar fears of the diminished possibilities for autonomy in European society and the growing alienation of people from themselves.

In fact, the flowering of the fairy tale in Europe and America during the latter half of the nineteenth century has a great deal to do with

alienation. As daily life became more structured, work more rational-
ized, and institutions more bureaucratic, there was little space left for
daydreaming and the imagination. It was the fairy tale that provided
room for amusement, nonsense, and recreation. This does not mean
that it abandoned its more traditional role in the civilizing process as
the agent of socialization. For instance, up until the 1860s the majority
of fairy-tale writers for children, including Catherine Sinclair, George
Cruikshank, and Alfred Crowquill in England; Carlo Collodi in Italy;
Comtesse Sophie de Ségur in France; and Heinrich Hoffmann and
Ludwig Bechstein in Germany, emphasized the lessons to be learned in
keeping with the principles of the Protestant ethic — industriousness,
honesty, cleanliness, diligence, virtuousness — and male supremacy.
However, just as the "conventional" fairy tale for adults had become
subverted at the end of the eighteenth century, there was a major
movement to write parodies of fairy tales, which were intended both
for children *and* adults. In other words, the classical tales were turned
upside down and inside out to question the value system upheld by the
dominant socialization process and to keep wonder, curiosity, and creativity alive. By the 1860s, it was clear that numerous writers were
using the fairy tale to subvert the formal structure of the canonized tales
as well as the governing forces in their societies that restricted free
expression of ideas. Such different authors as William Makepeace
Thackeray ("Bluebeard's Ghost," 1843), Nathanel Hawthorne
("Mosses from an Old Manse," 1846), Theodor Storm ("Hinzelmeier,"
1857), Mor Jokai ("Barak and His Wives," c. 1858), Gottfried Keller
("Spiegel the Cat," 1861), Edouard-René Laboulaye ("Zerbin the
Wood-Cutter," 1867), Richard Leander ("The Princess with the Three
Glass Hearts," 1871), George MacDonald ("The Day Boy and the
Night Girl," 1879), Catulle Mendés ("The Sleeping Beauty," 1885),
Mary De Morgan ("The Three Clever Kings," 1888), Oscar Wilde
("The Fisherman and His Soul," 1891), Robert Louis Stevenson ("The
Bottle Imp," 1892), and Hugo von Hofmannsthal ("The Fairy Tale of
the 672nd Night," 1895) were all concerned with exploring the poten-
tial of the fairy tale to reform both the prescripted way it had become
cultivated and the stereotypes and prejudices in regard to gender and
social roles that it propagated. The best example of the type of subver-

sion attempted during the latter part of the nineteenth century is Lewis Carroll's *Alice's Adventures in Wonderland* (1865), which has had a major influence on the fairy-tale genre up to the present.

Although many of the fairy tales were ironic or ended on a tragic note, they still subscribed to the utopian notion of the transformation of humans, that is, the redemption of the humane qualities and the overcoming of bestial drives. In America, for instance, Frank Stockton, who could be considered the "pioneer" writer of the fairy tale in America, and Howard Pyle, one of the finest writer-illustrators of fairy tales, touch upon the theme of redemption in their tales "The Griffin and the Minor Canon" (1885) and "Where to Lay the Blame" (1895). But the most notable American fairy tale of the nineteenth century was L. Frank Baum's *The Wonderful Wizard of Oz* (1900), which depicts Dorothy's great desire and need to break out of Kansas and determine her own destiny, a theme that Baum also explored in "The Queen of Quok" in *American Fairy Tales* (1901).

By the beginning of the twentieth century, the fairy tale had become fully institutionalized in Europe and America, and its functions had shifted and expanded. The institutionalization of a genre means that a specific process of production, distribution, and reception has become regularized within the public sphere of a society and plays a role in forming and maintaining the cultural heritage of that society. Without such institutionalization in advanced industrialized and technological countries, the genre would perish. Thus the genre itself becomes a kind of self-perpetuating institute involved in the socialization and acculturation of readers. It is the interaction of writer, publisher, and audience within a given society that makes for the definition of the genre in any given epoch. The aesthetics of each fairy tale will depend on how and why an individual writer wants to intervene in the discourse of the genre as institution.

By the beginning of the twentieth century the fairy tale as institution had expanded to include drama, poetry, ballet, music, and opera. In fact, one could perhaps assert that the pageants at the various European courts in the sixteenth and seventeenth centuries, especially the court of Louis XIV, had actually influenced and helped further the development of the literary fairy tale. Certainly, after André-Ernest

Modeste Grétry's *Zémire et Azore* (1771), based on "Beauty and the Beast," and Wolfgang Amadeus Mozart's *The Magic Flute* (1790), fairy-tale themes became abundant in the musical world of Europe in the nineteenth century as can be seen in E. T. A. Hoffmann's own *Undine* (1814), Gioacchino Rossini's *La Cenerentola* (1817), Robert Schumann's *Kreisleriana* (1835–40), Léo Delibes's *Coppélia* (1870), Peter Ilyich Tschaikovsky's *Sleeping Beauty* (1889) and *Nutcracker Suite* (1892), Engelbert Humperdinck's *Hänsel and Gretel* (1890), and Jacques Offenbach's *The Tales of Hoffmann* (1890). Again, the manner in which the fairy tale incorporated other art forms into its own institution reveals the vital role that adults have played in maintaining the genre. Never has the fairy tale ever lost its appeal to adults, and the fairy tale for adults or mixed audiences underwent highly significant changes in the twentieth century.

During the first half of the century, the major shift in the function of the literary tale involved greater and more explicit politicization. In France, Apollinaire, who wrote "Cinderella Continued" (1918), joined a group of experimental writers, who published their fairy tales in *La Baionette* to comment on the ravages of World War I. Hermann Hesse, who had written "The Forest Dweller" (1917–18) to criticize the conformity of his times, also published "Strange News From Another Planet" in 1919 to put forward his pacifist views. Thomas Mann also made a major contribution to the fairy-tale novel with *The Magic Mountain* (1924), which is filled with political debates about nationalism and democracy. Moreover, there was a wave of innovative and expressionist fairy tales in Germany written by Edwin Hoernle, Hermynia zur Mühlen, Mynona, Franz Hessel, Kurt Schwitters, Oskar Maria Graf, Bertolt Brecht, Alfred Döblin, and others who were politically tendentious. In England, the experimentation was not as great. Nevertheless, a volume entitled *The Fairies Return, Or, New Tales for Old* appeared in 1934 and contained tales with unusual social commentary by A. E. Coppard, Lord Dunsany, Eric Linklater, Helen Simpson, Edith Anna Œnone Somerville, Christina Stead, and G. B. Stern. Of course, after the Nazi rise to power and during the Spanish Civil War, the fairy tale became more and more the means to convey political sentiments. In Germany, the fairy tale was interpreted and produced according to Nazi ideology, and there are numerous examples of *völkisch* and fascist fairy-tale products. These, in turn, brought out a response of writers opposed to Nazism such as American H. I. Phillips's "Little Red Riding Hood as a Dictator Would Tell It" (1940).

Germany offers an extreme case of how the fairy tale became politicized or used for political purposes. But this extreme case does illustrate a general trend in the political intonation of fairy tales that continued into the 1940s and 1950s. For example, a work like J. R. R. Tolkien's *The Hobbit* (1938) was written with World War I in mind and with the intention of warning against a second world war. James Thurber's "The Girl and the Wolf" (1939) focused on power and violation. Georg Kaiser's "The Fairy Tale of the King" (1943) reflected upon dictatorship. Erich Kästner's "The Fairy Tale about Reason" (1948) projected the possibility of world peace. Ingeborg Bachmann's "The Smile of the Sphinx" (1949) recalled the terror of the Holocaust.

Once again, following World War II, the fairy tale set out to combat terror, but this time the terror did not concern the inhibitions of the civilizing process, rationalization, and alienation but rather the demented and perverse forms of civilization that had in part caused atrocities and threatened to bring the world to the brink of catastrophe. Confronted with such an aspect at the onset of the Cold War with other wars to follow, some writers like Henri Pourrat (*Le Trésor des Contes*, 1948–62) and Italo Calvino (*Fiabe Italiene*, 1956) sought to preserve spiritual and communal values of the oral wonder tales in revised versions, while numerous other writers drastically altered the fairy tale to question whether the utopian impulse could be kept alive and whether our sense of wonderment could be maintained. If so, then the fairy tale had to deal with perversity and what Hannah Arendt called the banality of evil. Writers like Philip K. Dick ("The King of the Elves," 1953), Naomi Mitchison ("Five Men and a Swan," 1957), Sylvia Townsend Warner ("Bluebeard's Daughter," 1960), Christoph Meckel ("The Crow," 1962), Stanislaw Lem ("Prince Ferix and the Princess Crystal," 1967), and Robert Coover ("The Dead Queen," 1973, and *Briar Rose*, 1996) provoke readers not by playing with their expectations but by disturbing their expectations. To a certain extent, they know that most of their readers have been "Disneyfied," that is, they have been subjected to the saccharine, sexist, and illusionary stereotypes of the Disney-culture industry. Therefore, these authors have felt free to explode the illusion that happy ends are possible in real worlds that are held together by the deceit of advertising and government. Especially since the 1970s and 1980s, the fairy tale has become more aggressive, aesthetically more complex and sophisticated, and more insistent on *not* distracting readers but helping them focus on key social problems and issues in their respective societies. This standpoint is especially apparent in the works of Janosch, Günter Kunert, Günter Grass, and Michael Ende in Germany; Michel Tournier, Pierre Gripari, and Pierrette Fleutiaux in France; Donald Bartheleme, Wendy Walker, Jane Yolen in the United States; Michael de Larrabeiti, Michael Rosen, and Peter Redgrove in Great Britain; and Gianni Rodari in Italy. Perhaps the major social critique carried by the fairy tale can be seen in the restructuring and reformation of the fairy tale itself as genre on the part of feminists. The result has been a remarkable production of nonsexist fairy tales for children and adults as well as theoretical works that explore the underlying implications of gender roles in fairy tales. Not only have individual writers such as Anne Sexton, Angela Carter, Olga Broumas, A. S. Byatt, Tanith Lee, Rosemarie Künzler, Jay Williams, and Robin McKinley created highly innovative tales that reverse and question traditional sex roles but also there have been collective enterprises in Italy, England, Ireland, and the United States that have reacted critically to the standard canon representing catatonic females flat on their backs waiting to be brought to life by charming princes. A good example is the work of Attic Press in Ireland, which has published such books as *Rapunzel's Revenge* (1985), *Cinderella on the Ball* (1991), and *Ride on Rapunzel* (1992). In a similar vein but with fairy tales much more diverse, Ellen Datlow and Terri Windling have published a series of important fairy-tale anthologies: *Black Thorn, White Rose* (1993), *Snow White, Blood Red* (1994), *Ruby Slippers, Golden Tears* (1995), and *Black Swan, White Raven* (1997). These books contain original stories by such notable writers as Joyce Carol Oates, John Crowley, Nancy Kress, Lisa Goldstein, Tanith Lee, and Gene Wolfe that break the parameters of the classical fairy tale and explore the genre's potential to address contemporary social concerns.

Of course, there are numerous fairy-tale works for adults that are blissfully serene and depict intact worlds that need no changing. Or there are placid revisions and patchwork reproductions of classical fairy tales meant to provide amusement or divertissement for readers and viewers. For instance there has been a great commercialization of the fairy tale since the 1950s that has led not only large publishers and corporations like Disney to profit from the classical prescription of seemingly innocuous doses of happy ends, but there have also been opportunistic books like James Garner's *Politically Correct Bedtime Stories* (1994) that mock politics and the fairy tale itself. Moreover, Jungian self-help books like Robert Bly's *Iron John* (1990) and Clarissa Pinkola Estés's *Women Who Run with the Wolves* (1993) soothe the souls of readers who are in need of spiritual nourishment. In all forms and shapes, the classical fairy tales continue to be moneymakers and thrive on basic sexist messages and conservative notions of social behavior. While the production of classical fairy-tale books continues to be a profitable enterprise — and publishers are often indiscriminate as long as the fairy tales are like money in the bank and produce a healthy interest — even more money is generated through fairy-tale films, plays, telecasts, and videos. The Faerie Tale Theatre, a television and video product created by Shelley Duvall, is a case in point.

The theatrical and cinematic use of the fairy tale is extremely significant since Western society has become more oriented toward viewing fairy-tale films, plays, and pictures rather than reading them. Here two fairy-tale productions in the United States might serve to illustrate a shift in function that is still in process. The 1987 Broadway musical of *Into the Woods*, an amusing collage of various fairy-tale motifs and characters, is typical of one aspect of the shift in function. It plays eclectically with all sorts of fairy-tale motifs and characters in a conventional Broadway-musical manner, and though there is a tragic side to the show, it arrives at a customary happy end to demonstrate how we can play with fairy-tale fragments to reshape the world in a tidy fashion. If it is true that the fairy tale in the seventeenth century was bound by the rules and regulations of court society that it largely served to represent court society to itself and to glorify the aristocracy, and if it is true that the social and political development in the nineteenth century set art free so that the fairy tale as genre became autonomous on the free market and in the public sphere, then it appears that there is a return, at least in theater, television, and cinema, to the representative function of the fairy tale. Of course, this time the society that is being represented to itself as glorious is the capitalist-consumer society with its "free" market system. In addition, the fairy tale implicitly and explicitly reflects the state's endeavors to reconcile divergent forces, to pacify discontents, to *show* how there are basically good elements within the bourgeois elite groups vying for control of American society, and these agents (often understood as heroes) are portrayed as seeking the happiness of *all* groups, especially the disenfranchised, who create the drama in real life and in the fairy-tale productions.

The 1987–89 television series of *Beauty and the Beast* is a good example of how the fairy tale as representation (and also legitimation) of elite bourgeois interests functions. No matter which thirty-minute sequel a viewer watches, the basic plot of this television adaptation of the classic tale follows the same lines: The young woman, Catherine, who is from the upper classes, devotes her talents to serving as a legal defender of the oppressed; and the Beast, Vincent, represents the homeless and the outcasts in America, forced to live underground. These two continually unite because of some elective affinity to oppose crime and corruption and clear the way for the moral forces to triumph in America. Though the different sequels do expose the crimes of the upper classes as well as the lower classes, the basic message is that there can be a reconciliation between beauty and beast, and we can live in a welfare state without friction.

Messages of reconciliation and elitism are clear in almost all the Disney cinematic productions of fairy tales from *Snow White and the Seven Dwarfs* (1937) to *Beauty and the Beast* (1993). With the possible exception of the innovative fairy-tale films produced by Jim Henson and Tom Davenport, the dominant tendency of most popular fairy-tale films for the big screen and television tend to follow the conventional patterns of the anachronistic classical fairy tales of Perrault, the Grimms, and Andersen, especially when the productions cater to children as consumers.

Despite the tendency of the film and television industry to use the fairy tale to induce a sense of happy end and ideological consent and to

mute its subversive potential for the benefit of those social groups controlling power in the public sphere, the fairy tale as institution cannot
be defined one-dimensionally or totally administered by its most visible
producers in the mass media and publishing. Writers, directors, and
producers are constantly seeking to revise classical fairy tales with
extraordinary films that address contemporary social issues. For
instance, Neil Jordan in *The Company of Wolves* (1984), an adaptation
of an Angela Carter story, and Matthew Bright in *Freeway* (1996) focus
on the nature of violation and rape in their films that deal with female
sexual desire and male sexual predatory drives. Implicit is a critique of
Little Red Riding Hood as a tale that suggests little girls want and cause
their own rape. Other filmmakers such as Mike Newell (*Into the West*,
1990) and John Sayles (*The Secret of Roan Innish*, 1993) have created
their own fairy-tale films based on Irish folklore that depict contemporary social predicaments critically while providing a means for viewers
to contemplate the stories with hope and a critical view toward the
future. All these filmmakers are seeking to redefine the fairy tale for
contemporary audiences in compelling ways.

Indeed, if we want to know what the fairy tale means today, then
we must take into consideration that the readers, viewers, and writers
of fairy tales constitute its broadest meaning, perhaps not in the old
communal way but in an individualized way that allows for free
expression and subversion of norms that are hypocritically upheld and
serve to oppress people. A good case in point here is Salman Rushdie's
inventive fairy-tale novel *Haroun and the Sea of Stories* (1990), which
concerns a young boy's quest to save his father's storytelling gifts that
are ultimately employed to undermine the oppression in the country
of Alifbay so ruinously sad that it had forgotten its name. Rushdie's
fairy tale allows him to diagnose the sickness of the country and
redeeming utopia by symbolically naming names without being concrete. While he himself is being oppressed, he has written a fairy tale,
which he wants passed on through the institution to urge readers to
question authoritarianism and to become inventive, daring, and cunning. He wants to leave his mark in society during troubled times by
providing hope for solutions without supplying the definitive answers.

This is also the case with Donna Napoli, who has written a series of
three fairy-tale novels for adolescents (*The Prince of the Pond: Otherwise*

Known as De Fawg Pin, 1993; *The Magic Circle*, 1993; and *Zel*, 1996)
that are subtle, poetic portrayals of young protagonists, who must
unravel the evil spells of bigotry and sadism to come into themselves.
While Napoli's protagonists unravel the mysteries of their lives, she
bases each novel on a classical fairy tale that she reweaves in highly
unique ways. In similar fashion, but in a more strident feminist fashion,
Emma Donoghue has questioned the stranglehold that classical tales
have on readers. *Kissing the Witch: Old Tales in New Skins* (1997) contains thirteen stunning first-person retellings of traditional tales that
consciously seek to upset reader expectations. For instance, Donoghue's
Cinderella narrator falls in love with a tender stranger who assumes the
role of her fairy godmother. A newlywed queen, who apparently is
doted on by her husband, learns that his love is like a cage that she
must flee. In all of Donoghue's tales, the protagonists come miracu-
lously to a new awareness that will stamp their lives, and her fairy tales
seek artfully to enter in and change the lives of her readers.

This is the ultimate paradox of the literary fairy tale: it wants to
mark reality without leaving a trace of how it creates the wondrous
effects. There is no doubt that the fairy tale has become totally institutionalized in Western society, part of the public sphere, with its own
specific code and forms through which we communicate about social
and psychic phenomena. We initiate children and expect them to learn
the fairy-tale code as part of our responsibility in the civilizing process.
This code has its key words and key marks, but it is not static. As in the
oral tradition, its original impulse of hope for better living conditions
has not vanished in the literary tradition, although many of the signs
have been manipulated in the name of male authoritarian forces. As
long as the fairy tale continues to awaken our wonderment and enable
us to project counterworlds to our present society, it will serve a meaningful social and aesthetic function not just for compensation but for
revelation: for the worlds portrayed by the best of our fairy tales are like
magic spells of enchantment that actually free us. Instead of petrifying
our minds, they arouse our imagination and compel us to realize how
we can fight terror and cunningly insert ourselves into our daily struggles and turn the course of the world's events in our favor.

two

The Rise of the French Fairy Tale and the Decline of France

Your people . . . whom you ought to love as your children, and who up to now have been passionately devoted to you, are dying of hunger. The culture of the soil is almost abandoned; the towns and the country are being depopulated; every trade is languishing and no longer supports the workers. All commerce is destroyed. . . . The whole of France is nothing but a huge hospital, desolated and without resources.
—Fénelon, *Letter to King Louis XIV*, 1694

U p until the 1690s, the oral folk tale in France had not been deemed worthy enough of being transcribed and transformed into literature, that is, written down and circulated among the literate people. In fact, with the exception of the significant collections of tales, *The Pleasant Nights* (1550–53) by Giovan Francesco Straparola and *Pentameron* (1634–36) by Giambattista Basile, in Italy, most of the European aristocracy and intelligentsia considered the folk tale beneath them. It was part of the vulgar, common people's tradition, beneath the dignity of cultivated people and associated with pagan beliefs and superstitions that were no longer relevant in Christian Europe. If the literate members of the upper classes did acknowledge the folk tale, it was only as crude entertainment, divertissement, anecdote, or homily in its oral form transmitted through such intermediaries as wet nurses, governesses, servants, peasants, merchants, and priests.

From the late Middle Ages up through the Renaissance, folk tales were told by nonliterate peasants among themselves at the hearth, in spinning rooms, or in the fields. They were told by literate merchants and travelers to people of all classes in inns and taverns. They were told by priests in the vernacular as part of their sermons to reach out to the peasantry. They were told to children of the upper clasess by nurses and governesses. They were remembered and passed on in different forms and versions by all members of society and told to suit particular occasions — *as talk*. But, gradually, this talk was elevated, cultivated, and made acceptable so it could enter into the French salons by the middle of the seventeenth century. Only by 1690, in fact, was it regarded worthy of print in France, and by 1696, there was a veritable vogue of printed fairy tales: The literary fairy tale had come into its own, and French aristocratic writers for the most part established the conventions and motifs for a genre that is perhaps the most popular in the Western world — and not only among children.

How did all this come about? Why the change in attitude toward the lowly oral folk tale? What kinds of literary fairy tales were created?

Though it is impossible to set a date for the rise of the literary fairy tale in France, such important studies as Roger Picard's *Les Salons littéraires et la société française 1610–1789* (1946), Marie Gougy-François's *Les grands salons feménins* (1965), Renate Baader's *Dames de Lettres* (1986), and Verena von der Heyden-Rynsch's *Europäische Salons* (1992) have shown that its origins can be located in the conversation and games developed by highly educated aristocratic women in the salons that they formed in the 1630s in Paris and that continued to be popular up through the beginning of the eighteenth century. Deprived of access to schools and universities, French aristocratic women began organizing gatherings in their homes to which they invited other women and gradually men in order to discuss art, literature, and topics such as love, marriage, and freedom that were important to them. In particular, the women wanted to distinguish themselves as unique individuals, who were above the rest of society and deserved special attention.

Generally speaking, these women were called *précieuses* and tried to develop a *précieux* manner of thinking, speaking, and writing to reveal and celebrate their innate talents that distinguished them from the vulgar and common elements of society. Most important here was the emphasis placed on wit and invention in conversation. The person who was a *précieux* (and numerous men were included in this movement) was capable of transforming the most banal thing into something brilliant and unique. Although there was a tendency among them to be effete and elitist, these women were by no means dilettantes. On the contrary, some of the most gifted writers of the time such as Mlle de Scudéry, Mlle de Montpensier, Mme de Sévigné, and Mme de Lafayette came out of this movement, and their goal was to gain more independence for women of their class and to be treated more seriously as intellectuals. In fact, one of the most important consequences of *préciosité* was its effect on women from the lower aristocracy and bourgeoisie, who were inspired to struggle for more rights and combat the rational constraints placed on their lives.

The women who frequented the salons were constantly seeking innovative ways to express their needs and to embellish the forms and style of speech and communication that they shared. Given the fact that they had all been exposed to folk tales as children and that they entertained themselves with conversational games that served as models for the occasional lyric and the serial novel, it is not by chance that they turned to the folk tale as a source of amusement. About the middle of the seventeenth century the aristocratic women started to invent parlor games based on the plots of tales with the purpose of challenging one another in a friendly fashion to see who could create the more compelling narrative. Such challenges led the women, in particular, to improve the quality of their dialogues, remarks, and ideas about morals, manners, and education and at times to question male standards that had been set to govern their lives. The subject matter of the conversations consisted of literature, mores, taste, love, and etiquette, whereby the speakers all endeavored to portray ideal situations in the most effective oratory style that would gradually be transformed into literary forms and set the standards for the *conte de fée* or what we now call the literary fairy tale.

By the 1670s there were various references in letters about the fairy tale as an acceptable *jeux d'esprit* in the salons. In this type of game, the women would refer to folk tales and use certain motifs spontaneously in their conversations. Eventually, they began telling the tales as a literary *divertimento, intermezzo,* or as a kind of after-dinner desert that one would invent to amuse listeners. This social function of amusement was complemented by another purpose, namely, that of self-portrayal and representation of proper aristocratic manners. The telling of fairy tales enabled women to picture themselves, social manners, and relations in a manner that represented their interests and those of the aristocracy. Thus, they placed great emphasis on certain rules of oration, such as naturalness and spontaneity, and themes, such as freedom of choice in marriage, fidelity, and justice. The teller of the tale was to make it "seem" as though the tale were made up on the spot and as though it did not follow prescribed rules. Embellishment, improvisation, and experimentation with known folk or literary motifs were stressed. The procedure of telling a tale as *bagatelle* (trinket or trifle) would work as follows: the narrator would be requested to think up a tale based on a particular motif; the adroitness of the narrator would be measured by the degree with which she was inventive and natural; the audience would respond politely with a compliment; then another member of the audience would be requested to tell a tale, not in direct competition with the other teller, but in order to continue the game and vary the possibilities for invention and symbolic expression that often used code words such as *galanterie, tendresse,* and *l'esprit* to signal the qualities that distinguished their protagonists.

By the 1690s the "salon" fairy tale became so acceptable that women and men began writing their tales down to publish them. The "naturalness" of the tales was, of course, feigned since everyone prepared tales very carefully and rehearsed them before participating in a particular salon ritual. Most of the notable writers of the fairy tale learned to develop this literary genre by going to the salons or homes of women who wanted to foster intellectual conversation. And some writers such as Mme D'Aulnoy, Mme de Murat, and Mlle L'Héritier even had their own salons. Moreover, there were festivities at King Louis XIV's court and at aristocratic homes, especially during the Car-

nival period, that people attended dressed as nymphs, satyrs, fawns, or
other fairy-tale figures. There were spectacular ballets and plays that
incorporated fairy-tale motifs as in the production of Molière and
Corneille's *Psyché* (1671), which played a role in the development of
the beauty and the beast motif in the works of Mme D'Aulnoy. In this
regard, the attraction to the fairy tale had a great deal to do with Louis
XIV, the Sun King's desire to make his court the most splendid and
radiant in Europe, for the French aristocracy and bourgeoisie sought
cultural means to translate and represent this splendor in form and
style to themselves and the outside world. Thus, the peasant contents
and the settings of the oral folk tales were transformed to appeal to
aristocratic and bourgeois audiences.

The transformation of the oral folk tale into a literary fairy tale was
not superficial or decorative. The aesthetics that the aristocratic
women developed in their conversational games and in their written
tales had a serious aspect to it: though they differed in style and content, these tales were all anticlassical and were implicitly written in
opposition to the leading critic of the literary establishment, Nicolas
Boileau, who championed Greek and Roman literature in the famous
"Quarrel of the Ancients and Moderns" (1687–96) as the models for
French writers to follow at that time. Instead, the early French fairy-
tale writers used models from French folklore and the medieval courtly
tradition. In addition, since the majority of the writers and tellers of
fairy tales were women, these tales displayed a certain resistance
toward male rational precepts and patriarchal realms by conceiving
pagan worlds in which the final "say" was determined by female fairies,
extraordinarily majestic and powerful fairies, if you will. To a certain
extent, *all* the French writers of fairy tales, men and women, "modern-
ized" an oral genre by institutionalizing it in literary form with utopian
visions that emanated from their desire for better social conditions
than they were experiencing in France at that time.

Despite the fact that their remarkable fairy tales set the tone and
standards for the development of most of the memorable literary fairy
tales in the West up to the present, they and their utopian visions are
all but forgotten, not only in English-speaking countries but also in
France itself. If anyone is known today and represents this genre, it is